Gluten Free
COOKBOOK

2000 Days of Easy and Flavorful Recipes to
Manage Celiac Disease, Cut Gluten, or
Simply for Healthy Eating

Diane Romano

2 Exclusive FREE Bonuses for You!

Don't forget to download them

Jump Now To the End of the Book
and scan the QR code!

CONTENTS

Introduction

Welcome to the delightful world of gluten-free cooking, where incredible flavors meet unbeatable nutrition in a dance of culinary joy. Whether you've chosen this path or necessity has guided you here, take heart—you are not alone! My venture into gluten-free living began many years ago when my daughter discovered her intolerance. It was a moment that changed our kitchen forever, transforming what felt like a formidable challenge into an exciting exploration of new tastes and textures.

This cookbook is born from countless experiments and delicious successes, crafted to show that living without wheat doesn't mean skimping on taste or variety. It's about discovering a whole new world of flavors and opportunities! Here, you'll find everything you need to elevate your gluten-free journey. From understanding celiac disease and gluten sensitivity to mastering delightful recipes for every occasion—be it a quick weekday meal or a lavish holiday feast.

Moreover, we've packed this book with practical tips to make gluten-free eating both affordable and simple for the entire family, turning what could be a daunting endeavor into a joyful experience. But this book isn't just a source of culinary inspiration; it's a beacon of encouragement. Life might throw challenges your way, whether it's cooking without wheat or facing other hurdles, but with dedication and creativity, anything is possible.

So, don your metaphorical apron with pride, embrace the adventure, and let's embark on this flavorful journey together. Here's to cooking, eating, and enjoying—gluten-free style! Bon appétit!

Understanding Gluten

Gluten—it's a word you've probably heard quite a bit recently, but what exactly is it? Simply put, gluten is a mixture of proteins found in grains like wheat, rye, and barley. It's the magic behind the chewy deliciousness of bread, giving dough its stretch and helping it rise during baking. But, as delightful as gluten can be for many, for those of us with celiac disease, it presents a serious challenge.

Celiac disease is an autoimmune disorder where even tiny amounts of gluten can cause damage to the small intestine. This damage interferes with absorbing nutrients from food, which can lead to malnutrition and, in severe cases, conditions like osteoporosis or even intestinal cancer. The symptoms of celiac disease can vary greatly—some might experience diarrhea, bloating, or abdominal pain, while others may feel fatigued or depressed, with no obvious physical signs, making it as tricky to diagnose as spotting Waldo in those beloved Where's Waldo books from our childhood.

If you suspect gluten might be affecting your health, don't hesitate to consult your doctor. It's important to catch these things early—after all, everyone deserves to enjoy good health, no matter their dietary restrictions. Let's not let gluten stand in the way!

Understanding the distinction between celiac disease and non-celiac gluten sensitivity is crucial for anyone navigating dietary challenges. If you suspect you might be suffering from either condition, it's imperative to seek advice from a healthcare professional for an accurate diagnosis. Contrary to popular belief, a

gluten-free diet is not merely a trendy choice or a quick fix for weight loss—it is an essential treatment for those diagnosed with either of these conditions. For them, avoiding gluten is the only way to maintain intestinal health and prevent the discomfort and potential harm caused by these conditions.

Interestingly, individuals with non-celiac gluten sensitivity may exhibit symptoms similar to those of celiac disease, such as digestive upset, after consuming gluten-containing foods, yet they do not suffer the same intestinal damage. This overlap can make diagnosis particularly challenging.

Embracing a gluten-free lifestyle can seem daunting at first, but it's truly about making informed choices and learning new habits. Mastering grocery shopping and cooking involves a keen eye for food labels to avoid hidden gluten in sauces, dressings, and other additives. However, there's a silver lining: you'll soon discover delicious alternatives like quinoa flour and almond meal, which open up a whole new world of baking—imagine whipping up scrumptious cakes and treats that everyone can enjoy, all without a trace of wheat.

In the next chapter, we'll dive deeper into gluten-free ingredients, exploring how they can transform your culinary repertoire and allow you to create delectable dishes that don't skimp on flavor or satisfaction. Let's continue this journey together, embracing the challenges and the joys of gluten-free cooking.

Gluten-Free Ingredients

Stepping through the doorway into the enchanting world of gluten-free cooking might seem like a journey into the unknown, but it's an adventure filled with endless culinary delights! This chapter is your guide to exploring an array of flavorful flours and vibrant ingredients that will breathe new life into your dishes.

Flours

At the heart of gluten-free cooking lies an incredibly versatile range of gluten-free flours, each with its own unique characteristics. Whether you're just beginning your gluten-free journey or you're a seasoned baker, the variety of flours available today ensures that you'll never run out of options or flavors.

Rice Flour: Ah, rice flour—where would we be without it? Whether it's white or brown rice you choose to grind, the result is a finely textured, delicately flavored powder. It's perfect for creating everything from fluffy cakes to tender pastries. I still cherish the memory of my first attempt at gluten-free Thanksgiving cookies made with rice flour; their delightfully crumbly texture was a genuine revelation!

Corn Flour: Also known as polenta, corn flour has been making waves as a fantastic gluten-free option. Derived from milled corn kernels, it imparts a rustic, earthy flavor that rice flour simply can't match. Whether you're baking muffins, breads, or even crepes, corn flour adds a touch of golden color and a satisfying crunch. Inspired by a Midwestern friend, I've mastered a cornbread recipe that's sure to become a staple in your kitchen as it has in mine.

Buckwheat Flour: Its name can be misleading, but buckwheat is completely unrelated to wheat. This robust grain, when ground into flour, offers a rich, nutty flavor that's a natural fit for pancake batter. Incorporating buckwheat pancakes into your breakfast menu is a must; they whisk me back to those cold winter mornings spent flipping flapjacks with my mom, a cherished ritual that filled our home with warmth and wonderful aromas.

Teff Flour: Originating from Ethiopia, teff flour is not only rich in protein, fiber, and iron but also boasts a sweet, nutty flavor that's ideal for baking breads, cakes, and cookies. Its versatility and nutritional profile make it a standout choice for any gluten-free pantry.

Amaranth Flour: Valued by the Aztecs and Maya, amaranth flour carries a slightly peppery taste that adds a fascinating twist to traditional baking. Try it in muffins or cookies and discover why this ancient grain was so revered.

Tapioca Flour: Derived from the cassava root, tapioca flour is a fantastic thickener for sauces, soups, and desserts. Its light texture and neutral flavor make it incredibly versatile, blending seamlessly into many dishes without altering their original taste profiles.

Other Gluten-Free Flours: Don't stop here; the world of gluten-free flours is vast and varied. From almond and quinoa to coconut flour, which I fell in love with during a memorable trip to Hawaii, each flour brings its own unique flavor and texture to the table. Coconut flour, in particular, has become a favorite in my summer baking—its light, tropical essence makes every bite a little celebration of sunshine.

Other Ingredients

Besides to the world of gluten-free flours, there's a treasure trove of other delightful and versatile gluten-free ingredients to explore, each ready to elevate your culinary creations.

Cornstarch: Cornstarch is a powerhouse thickener for soups and sauces and shines as a breading for frying. Imagine encasing your chicken in a layer of cornstarch to achieve that perfectly crunchy, golden crust—it's a game-changer for anyone craving that satisfying crunch.

Potato Starch: For those dreaming of airy, light textures in baked goods, potato starch is your secret weapon. But its magic doesn't stop there; it's also ideal for creating silky smooth sauces and heavenly light desserts. Have you ever tried making gnocchi at home? With potato starch, you can whip up a batch that rivals any high-end restaurant, right from your own kitchen.

Gluten-Free Yeast: For leavening, gluten-free options like brewer's yeast and gluten-free sourdough starters are invaluable. Whether you're crafting airy breads or rustic sourdough, these alternatives ensure that your baked goods are both delicious and gluten-free. Embarking on sourdough baking can be a challenge—as I discovered during the pandemic lockdown. It required patience and perseverance, but mastering it brought immense satisfaction and truly unbeatable flavors.

Basic Gluten-Free Ingredients: Never underestimate the power of essentials like eggs, gluten-free milk, and vegetable oil. Eggs are fundamental in gluten-free baking, helping to bind ingredients and enrich textures. For those avoiding dairy, almond or rice milk makes a fantastic substitute, blending seamlessly into your recipes. And when it comes to versatility, vegetable oil is a hero—perfect for frying or just drizzling over a salad for that extra touch of zest. I owe a nod to my vegan friend who introduced me to the wonders of coconut oil—it's a revelation!

Gluten-free cooking is more than managing dietary restrictions; it's an opportunity to innovate and play with flavors and textures. Don't hesitate to experiment with these foundational ingredients. Who knows what culinary masterpieces you might create? Let your imagination soar, embrace the adventure, and remember, you've got this!

The Art of Substitutions

In this chapter, we dive deep into the heart of gluten-free cooking: the art of substitutions. That's right—there's no need to abandon your beloved recipes just because they contain gluten. With a plethora of gluten-free alternatives available, you can continue to enjoy your favorite dishes, just with a little twist!

Common Substitutions

Wheat Flour: If you're mourning the loss of wheat in your diet, fear not. A rich variety of gluten-free flours awaits your culinary creativity. From the nutty depths of almond flour to the tropical lightness of coconut flour, and the traditional feel of rice and corn flours, each brings a unique flavor and textural profile to your dishes. Since gluten-free flours often absorb more liquid than their wheat counterparts, a good rule of thumb is to start with 1.25 times the amount of gluten-free flour compared to the wheat flour originally called for in your recipe. Experiment and adjust to find the perfect balance for your culinary creations.

Bread: Who says you can't have delicious bread on a gluten-free diet? The days of limited bread and pasta options are over. In your own kitchen, you can create mouthwatering gluten-free bread using a blend of the flours we've discussed. Remember to incorporate leavening agents like yeast or baking powder to help your bread rise. For that desired elastic texture reminiscent of glutenous bread, don't forget to add binders such as xanthan gum or psyllium husk. A basic guideline to transform any bread recipe is: 1 cup of gluten-free flour blend, 1 teaspoon of xanthan gum or psyllium husk, and 1 teaspoon of yeast for every cup of wheat flour you're replacing.

Pasta: The world of pasta just got more exciting with gluten-free options such as rice, corn, and lentil noodles. Each type offers a distinctive texture and flavor that can elevate any meal from ordinary to extraordinary. When substituting traditional pasta, the conversion is wonderfully simple: a one-for-one ratio. However, keep in mind that gluten-free pasta tends to cook quicker than traditional pasta, so watch it closely. Aim for al dente perfection to avoid a mushy meal.

Pizza: Pizza, a universal favorite, often comes laden with gluten in its traditional form. However, for those embracing a gluten-free lifestyle, fear not! Crafting a delicious gluten-free pizza at home is not only possible but can be a delightful culinary experiment. Start with a base made from gluten-free flours such as rice, almond, or quinoa flour. For convenience, you can also opt for pre-made gluten-free pizza bases available in stores.

Sauces and Dressings: Navigating sauces and dressings without gluten is easier than you might think. For instance, opt for tamari instead of regular soy sauce, as it is naturally gluten-free and avoids wheat-based contamination. If you're craving a creamy dressing, use cornstarch or rice flour as a thickener instead of wheat flour. Keeping these gluten-free staples in your pantry means you can whip up delicious, safe sauces and dressings with minimal effort.

Beer: Beer traditionally contains gluten, but the market has responded with a variety of gluten-free options, using grains like sorghum or millet instead of barley. If you're seeking a simpler alternative, cider is a fantastic choice, as it's naturally gluten-free. However, be wary of beverages labeled as "low-gluten"—these may still contain trace amounts of gluten. Always read labels carefully to ensure what you're consuming is truly gluten-free.

Breakfast Cereals: Many breakfast cereals are culprits for hidden gluten, but thankfully, the range of gluten-free options is growing. Look for cereals made from corn, rice, or quinoa. Always check the packaging to confirm they are certified gluten-free, ensuring a safe start to your day.

Top 10 Secrets to Adapting Your Recipes

Diving into gluten-free cooking doesn't mean giving up on your cherished culinary classics. It's about embarking on a delicious adventure, transforming the familiar into something extraordinary without gluten. As you learn to adapt your favorite recipes, you'll discover new flavors, enhance textures, and master techniques that make every dish a celebration. Prepare to recreate the meals you love with a twist that's not only safe but also thrillingly tasty. Let's unlock the secrets to successful gluten-free adaptations, ensuring that every bite remains a joyous experience.

1. **Experiment with different flours:** In the world of gluten-free baking, understanding the unique properties of different flours is essential for culinary success. Rice flour, with its light and neutral profile, is ideal for delicate baked goods, providing a subtle sweetness and airy texture. On the other hand, almond flour offers a richer, nuttier flavor and a denser, moister consistency, making it perfect for heartier recipes like brownies and bread. Mastering gluten-free baking involves not just choosing the right flour but often blending various types to achieve the perfect balance of flavor, moisture, and structure. For example, while rice flour excels in light cakes, it may need the support of almond flour to add the necessary body to more substantial dishes. This approach of mixing and matching flours encourages experimentation and leads to the discovery of optimal combinations that ensure your gluten-free dishes are just as delightful as their traditional counterparts.

2. **Adjust the amounts of liquids:** When working with gluten-free flours, you'll often notice that they absorb more liquid than traditional wheat flours. This can result in doughs and batters that are unexpectedly dry, making it tricky to achieve the desired texture in your baked goods. To counteract this, it's important to be flexible with your liquid measurements. Adding a bit more liquid—be it water, milk, or another appropriate wet ingredient—can help bring your mixture to the right consistency. The key is to add these additional liquids gradually as you mix, allowing you to observe the changes in texture and ensure that your batter or dough remains pliable and moist, without becoming overly wet. This adjustment is crucial for ensuring that your gluten-free creations are just as delicious and texturally pleasing as those made with wheat flour.

3. **Don't forget binding agents:** Achieving the desirable stickiness and elasticity that gluten typically provides can be a challenge. This is where binding agents like xanthan gum or psyllium become invaluable. These ingredients play a crucial role in mimicking the texture and cohesiveness that gluten imparts to baked goods. Xanthan gum, for instance, helps to prevent ingredients from separating and improves the texture by making it stretchier and more dough-like. Psyllium, on the other hand, not only aids in binding but also contributes additional fiber, enhancing the nutritional profile of your treats. Integrating these binding agents into your gluten-free recipes ensures that your baked goods maintain a satisfying chew and don't crumble, making them both delicious and structurally sound. This subtle adjustment is key to transforming your gluten-free baking from good to great, allowing you to enjoy wholesome, well-textured treats that closely resemble their gluten-containing counterparts.

4. **Check the cooking:** Monitoring cooking times is particularly critical when baking gluten-free goods, as they can behave quite differently in the oven compared to their gluten-containing counterparts. Gluten-free ingredients tend to cook faster, which can lead to unexpectedly quick browning and drying out if not carefully watched. To achieve perfectly baked outcomes, it's essential to remain vigilant while your dishes are in the oven. Setting a timer for a few minutes less than the recipe suggests can be a good starting point, allowing you to check the progress and adjust the time as needed. This practice helps prevent overcooking, ensuring that your gluten-free baked goods retain their desired moisture and texture. Keeping a close eye on the oven and making adjustments based on what you observe is key to mastering the art of gluten-free baking, leading to delicious and satisfying results every time.

5. **Cover to maintain moisture:** Maintaining moisture in gluten-free baked goods can be a bit of a challenge, as they tend to dry out more quickly than their gluten-containing counterparts. A simple yet effective way to address this issue is to cover your baking dish with aluminum foil during part of the cooking process. This technique helps to trap steam and moisture within the dish, preventing the exterior of your baked goods from becoming too dry or hard too soon. By covering your creations, especially towards the end of the baking time, you allow the interior to cook through without losing that tender, moist texture that makes baked treats so delightful. This approach is particularly beneficial for larger items like breads or cakes, where the surface can become overly browned or crusty before the middle has fully cooked. Adjusting the time you keep the dish covered can fine-tune the balance between a moist interior and a perfectly baked exterior, leading to consistently better results in your gluten-free baking endeavors.

6. **Experiment and have fun:** Embracing gluten-free cooking is all about experimentation and enjoying the process. Don't hesitate to try new approaches and learn from the inevitable mistakes along the way, as each step is an opportunity to grow as a cook. Seeing these culinary experiments as fun rather than a chore can transform your cooking experience, encouraging creativity and innovation. Remember, you're not alone on this journey; there's plenty of support and resources available to help you refine your gluten-free cooking skills. Embrace the adventure with an open mind and enjoy the process of discovery and learning in your kitchen.

7. **Use a mix of flours:** Using a mix of gluten-free flours is a great strategy for achieving the complex flavors and textures often associated with traditional wheat flour. By combining different gluten-free flours, you can tailor your baking blends to suit various recipes, enhancing both taste and texture. Here are some general guidelines on proportions for mixing these flours, designed to inspire your gluten-free baking adventures:

   Rice Flour, Potato Flour, and Tapioca Flour Mix: For a light and neutral blend, use 1 part rice flour, 1 part potato flour, and 1 part tapioca flour. This balanced mix is perfect for a wide range of baked goods, from fluffy cakes to tender cookies and bread.

   Almond Flour, Coconut Flour, and Tapioca Flour Mix: Create a richer, denser blend with 1 part almond flour, 1 part coconut flour, and 1 part tapioca flour. This mix is excellent for desserts that benefit from a moist and flavorful texture, such as cakes and muffins.

   Buckwheat Flour, Rice Flour, and Amaranth Flour Mix: For a robust and earthy blend, combine 1 part buckwheat flour, 1 part rice flour, and 1 part amaranth flour. This hearty combination is ideal for savory baked goods like bread and focaccia, adding depth and a wholesome bite.

   Quinoa Flour, Rice Flour, and Potato Flour Mix: To achieve a unique flavor with a light texture, mix 1 part quinoa flour, 1 part rice flour, and 1 part potato flour. This blend works well for lighter baked goods such as muffins and pancakes, offering a subtle, distinctive taste.

   Bean Flour, Rice Flour, and Corn Flour Mix: For a mix with a rich flavor and a heavier texture, use 1 part bean flour, 1 part rice flour, and 1 part corn flour. This combination works well for savory items like bread and tortillas, where a denser, more flavorful texture is desirable.

   These ratios are starting points and can be adjusted based on your specific baking needs and personal taste preferences. Experimenting with these blends will help you discover the perfect mix for your gluten-free recipes, allowing you to recreate the beloved textures and flavors of traditional baking without gluten.

8. **Add Extra Protein:** Flours like bean or lentil not only increase the protein content of your dishes but also enrich the flavor, adding depth to your culinary creations.

9. **Explore New Cooking Techniques:** Since gluten-free recipes respond differently than those containing wheat, experimenting with methods such as lowering the oven temperature for cookies or creating a humid environment for breads can make a significant difference. These adjustments help maintain moisture, enhance texture, and ensure proper rise, leading to delicious outcomes. By experimenting and observing the effects of these changes on your baked goods, you'll refine your methods and find the best ways to produce delightful gluten-free dishes. This process not only improves your results but also broadens your understanding of gluten-free baking dynamics.

10. **Don't forget about flavor:** It's essential to focus on texture and structure when making gluten-free dishes, but don't forget the flavor! Adding herbs, extracts, spices or other seasonings can take your meal from good to great. It's important that you put as much thought into the taste of your creation as its physical form.

With these secrets in your culinary arsenal, you're well-equipped to tackle gluten-free cooking with confidence and creativity. Embrace these tips, and you'll find that your gluten-free dishes are not just good alternatives but standouts in their own right. Enjoy the journey, and may your kitchen be filled with joy and delectable aromas!

Managing the Diet

Living gluten-free isn't just a personal journey; it's an adventure that can bring the whole family together. My path to gluten-free living began not for myself but for my dear daughter. Many years ago, we discovered she was gluten intolerant, which initially cast a shadow of confusion and worry over our family. However, we quickly saw this as an opportunity to come together, becoming more mindful of our diets and finding joy in our new culinary discoveries.

It's crucial to educate everyone in the household about what it means to live gluten-free and why it's necessary, particularly if the diet isn't universal. Understanding each other's needs fosters a supportive, harmonious environment. When I explained my daughter's condition to our family, they were not just understanding but also eager to help in managing her diet, ensuring that living gluten-free felt inclusive rather than isolating.

We've learned that openness about dietary restrictions, coupled with ensuring our meals are delightful for everyone, is key to family unity. It's about embracing food as a source of connection rather than seeing it as a divider due to different eating habits or dietary needs. We organize our pantry with a designated "gluten-free corner," clearly labeled to prevent any cross-contamination. This simple organization helps maintain a safe and inviting kitchen for everyone.

Meal planning also plays a crucial role. By preparing dishes everyone can enjoy—making the main course entirely gluten-free and varying the sides—we cater to all preferences at the table. This approach not only meets everyone's nutritional needs but also simplifies meal preparation. It shows that with a bit of creativity and care, a gluten-free lifestyle can enrich your family's life, bringing everyone closer through the shared experience of good, wholesome food.

Embracing a gluten-free lifestyle isn't just a necessity—it's an exciting opportunity. When I discovered my daughter was gluten intolerant many years ago, it felt like a door had opened, not closed. This revelation rekindled my passion for cooking, allowing me to create meals that not only satisfy the palate but also nurture the body. Now, every dish I serve is a celebration of both health and flavor, enjoyed by everyone at our family table.

Setting a positive example is crucial. Staying motivated and committed to this lifestyle change can inspire your family to embrace it alongside you. Since adopting a gluten-free diet for my daughter, our family dynamic has transformed. We communicate more openly, understand each other's needs better, and enjoy the creativity sparked by experimenting with new recipes. This journey has enriched our lives in ways we never imagined, bringing us closer together.

Celebrating the small victories is key to maintaining morale. Whether it's discovering a delightful new gluten-free biscuit or mastering a recipe that everyone loves, each achievement is a milestone. I still cherish the memory of baking my first loaf of gluten-free bread with my daughter. Though it wasn't perfect, the pride and joy we felt in that achievement were profound. We savored every slice, celebrating our effort as much as the taste.

Navigating dietary restrictions within your family may seem daunting, but doggedly, an open mind, and strong support from loved ones, you'll find that this new way of eating can be both manageable and enjoyable. So, wear your metaphorical apron with pride and tackle this challenge with enthusiasm. Before you know it, these moments of adaptation will not just be routine but moments of joy and discovery for the whole family.

Avoiding Cross-Contamination

Those who embrace a gluten-free lifestyle must remain hyper-vigilant to avoid any cross-contamination, as even the slightest presence of gluten can result in significant problems for individuals with intolerances. Here are some practical steps to ensure your kitchen remains a safe space for gluten-free cooking:

1. **Get Organized:** Dedicate specific areas of your kitchen for gluten-free meal preparation. This might mean separate shelves in the refrigerator, dedicated drawers in your pantry, or even a separate set of cooking tools like knives, cutting boards, and pots. If you have only one toaster, consider using toaster bags to keep gluten-free items safe. Always start with a clean work area to whip up your gluten-free delights.

2. **Label Everything:** Mark all your gluten-free items clearly with "Gluten-Free" labels. This practice not only helps in keeping them separate from gluten-containing foods but also prevents accidental mix-ups. Make it a family rule to respect these labels to avoid any unintended gluten consumption.

3. **Avoid Surface Contamination:** Always clean work surfaces, utensils, and kitchen equipment thoroughly after they have been in contact with gluten. Use hot water and soap, or place items in the dishwasher to ensure all gluten traces are removed, safeguarding your gluten-free cooking environment.

4. **Be Mindful of Ingredients:** Always read labels carefully to check for any hidden gluten or potential contamination. Ingredients like salad dressings can sometimes contain gluten without it being obvious. Whenever possible, choose products that are certified gluten-free for extra safety.

5. **Communicate with Your Family:** Regularly remind your family about preventing cross-contamination. Explain the precautions for handling gluten-containing foods and how they can support your gluten-free diet. A strong sense of responsibility ensures that everyone is meticulous when cooking and cleaning in the kitchen.

6. **Avoid Double-Dipping:** Never use the same frying oil, pasta water, or utensils for both gluten-free and gluten-containing foods. These small traces of gluten can cause adverse reactions. Always use separate tools and ingredients to maintain a strict gluten-free environment.

By following these steps, you can create a safe and inclusive kitchen that respects your gluten-free needs while still catering to the preferences of everyone in your household. Let's make your kitchen a worry-free zone where health and flavor meet in every gluten-free dish you prepare!

Smart Savings

With some smart planning and savvy shopping strategies, it's possible to follow a gluten-free lifestyle and save money concurrently. To get started on your budget-friendly journey, I'll give you some top tips as well as show you where to find all the best bargains. So if living life sans gluten doesn't have to mean emptying your wallet either - let's get saving!

Savvy Saving Tips

Navigating a gluten-free lifestyle doesn't have to be a strain on your wallet. Here are some savvy tips to help you save money while enjoying a delicious and diverse diet:

1. **Opt for Economical Gluten-Free Carbs:** When it comes to grains, it's smart to be budget-conscious. Corn, rice, and gluten-free oats are not only affordable but also versatile enough to serve as the foundation for countless meals. Next time you're at the store, consider these cost-effective options for your pantry staples.

2. **Choose Naturally Gluten-Free Foods:** Why spend extra on processed foods when nature offers a bounty of gluten-free options? Fruits, vegetables, tofu, nuts, and legumes are not only naturally free of gluten but are also packed with essential nutrients. They're generally less expensive than packaged gluten-free products. Integrating these into your meals as much as possible can offer significant savings.

3. **Bake Your Own Gluten-Free Goods:** Baking at home allows you to control your ingredients and cut costs. With a little practice, you can make homemade gluten-free bread, cookies, and other baked treats that are both satisfying and budget-friendly. There's a special joy in enjoying something delicious that you made yourself.

4. **Freeze Extra Meals and Snacks:** Doubling up on recipes when you cook is a great way to save both time and money. Prepare an extra batch of gluten-free lasagna or any other dish, and freeze it for later. This strategy is perfect for those busy days when cooking a fresh meal is too much of a hassle.

5. **Buy in Bulk:** Stocking up on staples like quinoa and lentils in bulk can lead to considerable savings, especially if you have a large family or consume these items regularly. Many stores offer discounts on bulk purchases, so take advantage of these deals whenever possible.

6. **Make Gluten-Free Meals a Family Affair:** Cooking separate meals can be time-consuming and costly. Instead, prepare delicious gluten-free dishes that everyone will love. This not only saves time but also educates your family about the gluten-free lifestyle and its benefits. Try making a gluten-free pizza night where everyone can choose their toppings, or a hearty salad packed with veggies, lean proteins, and a scrumptious gluten-free dressing. For dessert, indulge in gluten-free brownies or a vibrant fruit salad that's sure to please everyone.

7. **Shop Smarter:** Always plan your meals and make a grocery list before shopping. This strategy prevents impulse buys and ensures you purchase only what you need, keeping your budget in check. For instance, if you're planning to bake a gluten-free cake, list all necessary ingredients beforehand. This focused approach to shopping helps avoid unnecessary purchases and saves money.

8. **Use Mainstream Gluten-Free Products:** Many everyday food products have gluten-free versions, often at competitive prices. Look for gluten-free cereals, chips, and crackers that are readily available in regular supermarkets. This eliminates the need for multiple shopping trips and can be handy for families with children who enjoy these snacks.

9. **Join Gluten-Free Facebook Groups:** Online communities are a treasure trove of information and support. Joining gluten-free Facebook groups allows you to stay updated on new products, special deals, and discounts. Plus, you can exchange tips and advice with others who understand the gluten-free lifestyle, making it easier to navigate.

10. **Avoid Food Waste:** Plan your meals around what you already have in your pantry and refrigerator to minimize waste and spending. Use up ingredients that are close to their expiration dates as the basis for your recipes. For example, if you have chicken that needs to be used, why not make a delicious gluten-free Thai green curry? This approach ensures you get the most out of your groceries and reduces food waste.

Hunting for Best Deals and Discount

Navigating the gluten-free landscape affordably involves a mix of smart shopping strategies that don't compromise on quality or variety. One effective way to save is by taking advantage of exclusive coupons offered by many gluten-free brands. For example, Enjoy Life frequently provides discounts like $1.50 off on two items, and similar savings can be found with brands such as Udi's, Franz, Glutino, Van's Lance, and Simple Mills. Regularly checking their websites for these deals can significantly reduce your grocery bills over time.

Another tip for keeping costs down is shopping at retailers known for their value. Walmart's Great Value brand, for instance, offers a range of gluten-free products that are both affordable and high quality. ALDI is another excellent option, especially if you're into baking or prefer ready-made gluten-free goods. Their liveGfree line is not only economical but also boasts a variety of top-notch ingredients that might surprise the discerning shopper.

For those who prefer the convenience of meal kits, Blue Apron offers a fantastic service that caters to gluten-free diets, complete with a $30 discount on your first order. They deliver straight to your door and allow customers to specify allergens, ensuring that your dietary needs are met without any hassle.

Trader Joe's and Costco are also great destinations for gluten-free shoppers. Trader Joe's has a fantastic selection of gluten-free products at reasonable prices, allowing you to explore a wide range of options without stretching your budget. If you're looking to buy in bulk, Costco offers substantial savings on gluten-free products, which is particularly beneficial for large families or frequent consumers of these products.

Overall, there are many options to save on gluten-free products. Whether you choose to search for online coupons, shop at specific brands, or buy in bulk, the important thing is that you don't have to compromise your health or well-being to save money. So, the next time you find yourself grocery shopping, remember these tips. You might be surprised at how much you can save.

Breakfast

Mango Smoothie Bowl

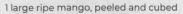

10 mn

0 mn

1-2

1. In a blender, combine the mango cubes, frozen banana slices, coconut milk, coconut yogurt, and honey or maple syrup if using. Blend until the mixture is smooth and creamy. If the smoothie is too thick, add a little more coconut milk to achieve your desired consistency.

2. Pour the smoothie mixture into a bowl. The beauty of a smoothie bowl is in its thick, spoonable texture, so aim for a consistency that will support your chosen toppings.

3. Arrange your toppings over the surface of the smoothie bowl. Create a visually appealing pattern with sliced almonds, fresh berries, coconut flakes and chia seeds. Serve immediately.

- 1 large ripe mango, peeled and cubed
- 1 medium banana, sliced and frozen
- ½ cup coconut milk (or any plant-based milk)
- 2 Tbsp. coconut yogurt
- 1 Tbsp. honey or maple syrup (optional, adjust to taste)
- Toppings: sliced almonds, fresh berries, coconut flakes, chia seeds

 (per serving, based on 2 servings):
Calories: 250, Protein: 3g, Carbohydrates: 35g, Fat: 12g, Fiber: 5g, Sugar: 25g

For an extra protein boost, consider adding a scoop of your favorite gluten-free protein powder to the blender before mixing.

Spinach and Feta Frittata

10 mn

30 mn

4-6

1. Preheat your oven to 375°F. In a large bowl, whisk together the eggs and almond milk until fully combined. Season with a pinch of salt and pepper.

2. Heat olive oil in a 10-inch oven-proof skillet over medium heat. Add the chopped onion and garlic, sautéing until translucent and fragrant.

3. To the skillet, add the chopped spinach, cooking just until wilted.

4. Pour the egg mixture over the sautéed onion, garlic, and spinach. Crumble the feta cheese evenly over the top. Let it cook without stirring for about 2-3 minutes, allowing the bottom to set slightly.

5. Transfer the skillet to the oven and bake for 20-25 minutes, or until the frittata is set and the top is lightly golden. Once done, let it cool for a few minutes. Garnish with cherry tomatoes and fresh herbs before serving.

- 8 large eggs
- ½ cup almond milk
- 1 Tbsp. olive oil
- 1 small onion, finely chopped
- 2 cloves garlic, minced
- 2 cups fresh spinach, roughly chopped
- ½ cup crumbled feta cheese (ensure it's gluten-free)
- Salt and pepper, to taste
- Optional: Cherry tomatoes for garnish, fresh herbs, for serving

 (per serving, based on 4 servings):
Calories: 280, Protein: 20g, Carbohydrates: 6g, Fat: 20g, Fiber: 1g, Sugar: 3g

Don't hesitate to mix in additional vegetables or swap the spinach for kale or Swiss chard.

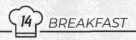

Chia and Almond Milk Pudding with Mixed Berries

10 mn*

0 mn

4

1. In a mixing bowl, combine the chia seeds, almond milk, maple syrup, vanilla extract, and a pinch of salt.
2. Cover the bowl with plastic wrap or a lid and refrigerate for at least 4 hours, preferably overnight.
3. While the pudding sets, prepare your mixed berries. If using strawberries, slice them to match the size of the other berries.
4. Once the chia pudding has set, give it a good stir to break up any clumps. Taste and add more maple syrup if you like it sweeter. Spoon the pudding into bowls or glasses, topping each with a generous helping of mixed berries. Garnish with mint leaves, a sprinkle of gluten-free granola, or a drizzle of honey if desired.

*plus at least 4 hours of chilling

- ½ cup chia seeds
- 2 cups unsweetened almond milk (ensure it's gluten-free)
- 2 Tbsp. maple syrup, plus more to taste
- 1 tsp. vanilla extract
- Pinch of salt
- 1 cup mixed berries for topping
- Optional garnishes: mint leaves, a sprinkle of gluten-free granola, or a drizzle of honey

 (per serving): Calories: 200, Protein: 5g, Carbohydrates: 25g, Fat: 10g, Fiber: 8g, Sugar: 10g

 Feel free to experiment with different types of milk, such as coconut or oat milk. For an extra layer of texture and flavor, layer the pudding and berries with gluten-free granola.

Buckwheat Crepes with Honeyed Ricotta and Sauteed Plums

15 mn*

20 mn

4

1. In a blender, combine the buckwheat flour, milk, eggs, salt, and melted butter or coconut oil. Blend until smooth. Let the batter rest for at least 30 minutes at room temperature. In a small bowl, mix the ricotta cheese with honey until well combined. Adjust the sweetness according to taste and set aside.
2. Heat a tablespoon of coconut oil or butter in a skillet over medium heat. Add the sliced plums and sprinkle with a little ground cinnamon. Sauté until the plums are tender and caramelized, about 5-7 minutes. Remove from heat and keep warm.
3. Heat a non-stick skillet or crepe pan over medium heat and lightly coat with butter or oil. Pour about ¼ cup of batter into the pan, tilting it to spread the batter thinly. Cook for about 1-2 minutes until the edges begin to lift, then flip and cook for another minute on the other side. Repeat with the remaining batter.
4. Spread a generous amount of the honeyed ricotta on half of each crepe, top with sautéed plums, then fold the crepe in half or roll it up. Repeat with the remaining crepes.
5. Drizzle with additional honey and serve warm, inviting each bite to be a delightful mix of nutty, sweet, and tart flavors.

*plus 30 minutes resting

- 1 cup buckwheat flour
- 1 ½ cups milk (any kind, dairy or plant-based)
- 2 large eggs
- A pinch of salt
- 1 Tbsp. melted butter or coconut oil, plus more for cooking
- 1 cup ricotta cheese
- 2 Tbsp. honey, plus more for drizzling
- 4 plums, pitted and sliced
- 1 Tbsp. coconut oil or butter, for sautéing
- A sprinkle of ground cinnamon, for the plums

 (per serving): Calories: 420, Protein: 15g, Carbohydrates: 50g, Fat: 20g, Fiber: 4g, Sugar: 25g

 If the batter seems too thick, adjust by adding a little more milk until you reach a thin, pourable consistency. For an extra touch of luxury, sprinkle toasted almond slices or walnuts over the crepes before serving.

Banana and Walnut Muffins

15 mn

20-25 mn

12

1. Start by preheating your oven to 350°F and preparing a muffin tin with paper liners or a light greasing. In a large mixing bowl, whisk together the flour, baking powder, baking soda, salt, and cinnamon. In a separate bowl, blend the mashed bananas, sugar, coconut oil, eggs, and vanilla extract until the mixture is smooth.

2. Combine the wet and dry ingredients, stirring just until they are integrated. Remember, a few lumps are okay; overmixing can make the muffins tough. Fold in the chopped walnuts, saving a handful to sprinkle on top of the muffins for a bit of extra crunch.

3. Evenly distribute the batter among the muffin cups, filling each about three-quarters full. If you like, sprinkle the top of each muffin with a bit more chopped walnuts and a dusting of sugar.

4. Bake in the preheated oven for 20-25 minutes or until a toothpick inserted into the center of a muffin comes out clean. Allow the muffins to cool in the pan for a few minutes before transferring them to a wire rack to cool completely.

- 2 cups GF all-purpose flour (ensure it includes xanthan gum for best results)
- 1 tsp. baking powder
- ½ tsp. baking soda
- ¼ tsp. salt
- ½ tsp. ground cinnamon
- 3 ripe bananas, mashed (about 1 cup)
- ¾ cup granulated sugar
- ⅓ cup melted coconut oil
- 2 large eggs, beaten
- 1 tsp. vanilla extract
- ½ cup chopped walnuts
- Optional: A sprinkle of GF granulated sugar

 (per muffin): Calories: 220, Protein: 3g, Carbohydrates: 30g, Fat: 10g, Fiber: 2g, Sugar: 15g

 Experimenting with add-ins like chocolate chips or a dash of nutmeg can add an exciting twist to your muffins. For a moister texture, consider incorporating a small amount of yogurt or applesauce into the batter.

Homemade Gluten-Free Granola

10 mn

25-30 mn

5 cups

1. Begin by preheating your oven to 300°F and lining a large baking sheet with parchment paper.

2. In a large bowl, mix the rolled oats, nuts, and seeds. In a separate small bowl, whisk together the melted coconut oil, maple syrup or honey, vanilla extract, salt, and cinnamon until well combined.

3. Pour the wet ingredients over the oat mixture and stir until everything is well coated. Spread the granola in an even layer on the prepared baking sheet.

4. Bake in the preheated oven for about 25-30 minutes, or until golden, stirring halfway through to ensure even baking. Let the granola cool completely on the baking sheet. It will crisp up as it cools. Once cooled, stir in the dried fruits (and coconut flakes or chocolate chips if using).

5. Store the granola in an airtight container at room temperature for up to 2 weeks.

- 3 cups GF rolled oats
- 1 cup mixed nuts, roughly chopped
- ½ cup mixed seeds
- ¼ cup coconut oil, melted
- 1/3 cup maple syrup or honey
- 2 tsp. vanilla extract
- ½ tsp. salt
- 1 tsp. ground cinnamon
- ½ cup dried fruits, chopped if large pieces
- Optional: coconut flakes, dark chocolate chips

 (per serving, ½ cup): Calories: 250, Protein: 6g, Carbohydrates: 28g, Fat: 14g, Fiber: 4g, Sugar: 9g

 For a clumpier granola, press the mixture firmly onto your baking sheet before baking and let it cool completely before breaking it into pieces.

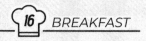

Savory Oatmeal with Spinach and Poached Egg

10 mn

15 mn

2

1. In a medium saucepan, bring the water or vegetable broth to a boil. Add the oats and salt, reducing the heat to a simmer. Cook, stirring occasionally, until the oats are soft and have absorbed the liquid, about 5-7 minutes.

2. While the oatmeal cooks, heat 1 tablespoon of olive oil in a skillet over medium heat. Add the spinach and sauté until just wilted, about 2-3 minutes. Season with a little salt to taste.

3. Bring a small pot of water to a gentle simmer and add a teaspoon of vinegar. Crack an egg into a small bowl and gently slide it into the simmering water. Repeat with the second egg. Poach the eggs for about 3-4 minutes, or until the whites are set but the yolks are still runny. Remove the eggs with a slotted spoon and set them on a paper towel to drain.

4. Divide the cooked oatmeal between two bowls. Top each with the sautéed spinach and a poached egg. Season with paprika, freshly ground black pepper, and an extra sprinkle of salt if needed.

5. Drizzle each serving with a bit more olive oil for richness and serve immediately.

- 1 cup GF rolled oats
- 2 cups water or vegetable broth
- ¼ tsp. salt, plus more to taste
- 1 Tbsp. olive oil, plus more for drizzling
- 2 cups fresh spinach, roughly chopped
- 2 large eggs
- tsp. vinegar (for poaching the eggs)
- Ground paprika, for garnish
- Freshly ground black pepper, to taste

(per serving): Calories: 350, Protein: 14g, Carbohydrates: 38g, Fat: 16g, Fiber: 6g Sugar: 1g

To elevate this dish even further, consider adding a sprinkle of grated Parmesan or a dash of hot sauce for an extra layer of flavor.

Quinoa and Apple Porridge

10 mn

25 mn

4

1. In a medium saucepan, combine the rinsed quinoa and 2 cups of almond milk. Bring to a boil over medium heat, then reduce the heat to low, cover, and simmer for 15 minutes, or until the quinoa is tender and most of the liquid has been absorbed.

2. Stir in the diced apples, maple syrup, cinnamon, and a pinch of salt into the quinoa. Continue to cook, uncovered, over low heat, stirring occasionally, for 5-10 minutes, or until the apples are soft and the porridge has thickened to your liking. The apples should be tender yet retain a slight bite.

3. If the porridge is too thick, add a little more almond milk until you reach your desired consistency. Taste and add more maple syrup if you prefer it sweeter.

4. Spoon the warm porridge into bowls. Top with your choice of chopped nuts, fresh berries, or a dollop of yogurt for an extra touch of creaminess and flavor.

5. Drizzle with a little more maple syrup or almond milk before serving, if desired.

- 1 cup quinoa (rinse thoroughly to remove the natural coating of saponins)
- 2 cups almond milk, plus more for serving
- 2 apples, peeled and diced (like Fuji or Honeycrisp)
- 2 Tbsp. maple syrup, plus more to taste
- ½ tsp. ground cinnamon
- Pinch of salt
- Optional toppings: chopped nuts, fresh berries, or a dollop of yogurt

(per serving): Calories: 250, Protein: 6g, Carbohydrates: 45g, Fat: 5g, Fiber: 5g, Sugar: 15g

For a seasonal twist, try incorporating pears instead of apples or adding a pinch of nutmeg alongside the cinnamon for extra warmth.

Vegetable Quiche

20 mn*

55 mn

6-8

*plus chilling

For the Crust:
- 1 ½ cups GF all-purpose flour
- ½ tsp. salt
- ½ cup cold butter, diced
- 4-6 Tbsp. ice water

For the Filling:
- 1 Tbsp. olive oil
- 1 small onion, diced
- 2 cloves garlic, minced
- 1 cup chopped spinach
- ½ cup diced bell peppers
- ½ cup sliced mushrooms
- ½ cup cherry tomatoes, halved
- 4 large eggs
- 1 cup milk or a dairy-free alternative
- 1 cup grated cheese (optional)
- Salt and pepper, to taste
- Herbs like thyme or basil, for garnish

1. In a large bowl, combine the gluten-free flour and salt. Add the cold, diced butter and use a pastry cutter or your fingers to work it into the flour until the mixture resembles coarse crumbs. Gradually add ice water, stirring until the dough comes together. Wrap in plastic and chill for at least 30 minutes. Preheat the oven to 375°F. Roll out the chilled dough on a floured surface and press it into a 9-inch pie dish. Prick the bottom with a fork, line with parchment paper, fill with pie weights or dried beans, and bake for 10 minutes. Remove the weights and bake for another 5 minutes until slightly golden.

2. Heat olive oil in a skillet over medium heat. Sauté the onion, garlic, spinach, bell peppers, and mushrooms until softened. Let cool slightly, then evenly distribute the vegetables and cherry tomatoes over the pre-baked crust.

3. In a bowl, whisk together the eggs, milk, and grated cheese (if using). Season with salt and pepper. Pour this mixture over the vegetables in the crust. Bake the quiche for 35-40 minutes, or until the custard is set and the top is golden brown. Let cool for a few minutes before slicing. Garnish with fresh herbs and serve warm.

(per serving, based on 8 servings): Calories: 350, Protein: 10g, Carbohydrates: 25g, Fat: 23g, Fiber: 3g, Sugar: 3g

Asparagus, leeks, or zucchini make great additions or substitutions. For a lighter version, substitute half of the eggs with egg whites and use a low-fat milk alternative.

Sweet Potato Pancakes

15 mn

20 mn

4

- 1 medium sweet potato, cooked and mashed (about 1 cup)
- 1 ¼ cups GF all-purpose flour
- 2 tsp. baking powder
- ½ tsp. ground cinnamon
- ¼ tsp. ground nutmeg
- ¼ tsp. salt
- 2 large eggs
- 1 cup almond milk (or any milk of your choice)
- 2 Tbsp. maple syrup, plus more for serving
- 1 tsp. vanilla extract
- Butter or coconut oil, for cooking

1. In a large mixing bowl, sift together the gluten-free flour, baking powder, cinnamon, nutmeg, and salt. In another bowl, whisk the mashed sweet potato, eggs, almond milk, maple syrup, and vanilla extract until well combined.

2. Gradually incorporate the dry ingredients into the wet mixture, stirring until just combined. Be careful not to overmix to keep the pancakes light and fluffy.

3. Heat a non-stick skillet or griddle over medium heat and lightly grease with butter or coconut oil.

4. Pour ¼ cup of batter for each pancake onto the skillet. Cook until bubbles form on the surface and the edges look set, about 2-3 minutes. Flip and cook for an additional 2 minutes or until golden brown and cooked through. Serve the pancakes warm, drizzled with maple syrup, and if desired, a sprinkle of cinnamon or a dollop of yogurt.

(per serving): Calories: 220, Protein: 6g, Carbohydrates: 40g, Fat: 4g, Fiber: 3g, Sugar: 10g

For an added nutritional boost, consider incorporating a tablespoon of flaxseed meal or chia seeds into the batter.

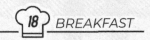

Coconut and Berry Smoothie Bowl

10 mn

0 mn

1-2

1. In a blender, combine the frozen mixed berries, coconut milk, coconut yogurt, frozen banana, chia seeds, and honey or maple syrup if using. Blend until smooth and creamy. If the mixture is too thick, add a little more coconut milk until you reach your desired consistency.

2. Pour the smoothie mixture into a bowl. The joy of a smoothie bowl lies in its creamy, spoonable texture, so aim for a thick consistency that will hold your toppings.

3. Artfully arrange your chosen toppings over the smoothie base. Mix textures and colors by adding fresh berries, banana slices, a sprinkle of shredded coconut, a handful of gluten-free granola, and a few more chia seeds for crunch. Finish with a final drizzle of honey or maple syrup for a touch of sweetness. Serve immediately, diving into a bowl that's a feast for the senses.

- 1 cup frozen mixed berries
- ½ cup coconut milk (use the thick part from the top of the can for extra creaminess)
- ¼ cup coconut yogurt
- 1 banana, sliced and frozen
- 1 Tbsp. chia seeds
- 1 Tbsp. honey or maple syrup (optional, for sweetness)
- Toppings: additional berries, sliced banana, shredded coconut and chia seeds

 (per serving, based on 2 servings):
Calories: 300, Protein: 4g, Carbohydrates: 35g, Fat: 18g, Fiber: 7g Sugar: 20g

 For an extra protein boost, consider adding a scoop of your favorite gluten-free protein powder to the smoothie blend.

Pear and Almond Butter Toast on Gluten-Free Bread

5 mn

5 mn

1-2

1. Toast the gluten-free bread to your liking, aiming for a golden-brown color and a slightly crispy texture. Spread a generous layer of almond butter on each slice of toasted bread.

2. Arrange the thinly sliced pear on top of the almond butter, covering the surface.

3. For a touch of added sweetness and flavor, drizzle the toast with honey or maple syrup, then sprinkle a bit of ground cinnamon over the top.

4. If desired, add a final layer of texture by sprinkling crushed almonds or a handful of gluten-free granola over the toast. Serve immediately.

- 2 slices of GF bread
- ¼ cup almond butter
- 1 ripe pear, thinly sliced
- A drizzle of honey or maple syrup (optional)
- A sprinkle of ground cinnamon
- A handful of crushed almonds or gluten-free granola for crunch (optional)

 (per serving, based on 2 servings): Calories: 250, Protein: 6g, Carbohydrates: 30g, Fat: 12g, Fiber: 5g, Sugar: 12g

 For an extra layer of flavor, consider toasting the almonds before crushing them for the topping.

10 mn

25 mn

4

- 1 cup millet, rinsed
- 4 cups water or milk
- A pinch of salt
- 2 Tbsp. coconut oil or butter
- 2 ripe bananas, sliced
- 2 Tbsp. brown sugar or maple syrup
- ½ cup pecans, roughly chopped
- A dash of ground cinnamon (optional)
- Additional honey or maple syrup, for serving

(per serving): Calories: 350, Protein: 6g, Carbohydrates: 50g, Fat: 14g, Fiber: 6g, Sugar: 15g

Millet Porridge with Caramelized Bananas and Pecans

1. In a medium saucepan, combine the millet, water or milk and a pinch of salt. Bring to a boil, then reduce the heat to low, cover, and simmer for about 15-20 minutes, or until the millet is tender and the liquid has been absorbed. Stir occasionally to prevent sticking and add more liquid if needed.

2. Heat the coconut oil or butter in a skillet over medium heat. Add the sliced bananas and sprinkle with brown sugar or drizzle with maple syrup. Cook for 2-3 minutes on each side, or until the bananas are golden and caramelized. Remove from heat and set aside.

3. In the same skillet, toast the chopped pecans over medium heat for about 3-5 minutes, stirring frequently, until they are fragrant and lightly browned. Be careful not to burn them.

4. Divide the cooked millet porridge between bowls. Top with the caramelized bananas, toasted pecans, and a dash of cinnamon if using. Drizzle with additional honey or maple syrup for added sweetness, if desired.

 For a creamier porridge, use almond milk or coconut milk

10 mn*

15 mn

2-4

assuming rice is pre-cooked and chilled

- 2 cups cooked and chilled rice (jasmine or basmati)
- 1 cup kimchi, chopped (ensure it's gluten-free)
- 2 Tbsp. kimchi juice (from the kimchi container)
- 2 Tbsp. coconut aminos or a GF soy sauce alternative
- 1 Tbsp. sesame oil
- 2 eggs, beaten
- ½ cup frozen peas and carrots, thawed
- 2 green onions, thinly sliced
- 1 Tbsp. vegetable oil
- Salt and pepper, to taste
- Optional toppings: sesame seeds, sliced green onions, or a fried egg

(per serving, based on 4 servings): Calories: 250, Protein: 7g, Carbohydrates: 38g, Fat: 8g, Fiber: 2g, Sugar: 2g

Kimchi Fried Rice

1. Heat vegetable oil in a large skillet or wok over medium-high heat. Add the peas and carrots, sautéing until they begin to soften, about 2-3 minutes.

2. Stir in the chopped kimchi and cook for another 2 minutes, allowing the flavors to meld.

3. Push the veggies and kimchi to the side of the pan. Pour the beaten eggs into the empty side, scrambling gently until they are just set.

4. Add the chilled rice, breaking up any clumps. Pour in the kimchi juice and coconut aminos, stirring to combine all the ingredients well. Cook for 5-7 minutes, or until the rice is heated through and slightly crispy. Drizzle sesame oil over the fried rice, and mix thoroughly. Season with salt and pepper to taste. Serve the kimchi fried rice hot, garnished with your favorite topping.

 Feel free to add more vegetables like bell peppers or mushrooms for additional texture and nutrients. If you enjoy extra heat, consider adding a tablespoon of gochujang (Korean chili paste).

Cowboy Breakfast Bowls

 15 mn

 25 mn

 4

1. Heat olive oil in a large skillet over medium heat. Add the diced potatoes, seasoning them with salt, pepper, paprika, and garlic powder. Cook until the potatoes are golden and crispy, about 10-15 minutes, stirring occasionally.

2. In another pan, cook the chopped bacon over medium heat until crisp. Remove the bacon and set it aside, leaving the bacon grease in the pan. In the same pan used for bacon, sauté the diced onion and bell pepper until soft and slightly caramelized, about 5-7 minutes.

3. Pour the beaten eggs over the sautéed onions and peppers, scrambling them together until the eggs are just set.

4. Assemble the breakfast bowls: Start with a base of crispy potatoes, then layer on the scrambled eggs with onions and peppers, and top with crispy bacon and shredded cheese. Garnish each bowl with sliced avocado and your choice of optional toppings. Serve hot.

- 2 large potatoes, diced into small pieces
- 4 slices of bacon, chopped
- 4 large eggs, beaten
- ½ cup shredded cheddar cheese
- 1 avocado, sliced
- 1 small onion, diced
- 1 bell pepper, diced
- 2 Tbsp. olive oil
- Salt and pepper, to taste
- 1 tsp. paprika
- ½ tsp. garlic powder
- Optional toppings: sliced green onions, chopped tomatoes, hot sauce, or salsa

 (per serving): Calories: 400, Protein: 18g, Carbohydrates: 30g, Fat: 24g, Fiber: 5g Sugar: 3g

 The potatoes can be roasted in the oven for a healthier option. Toss them with olive oil and seasonings, then roast at 425°F until crispy, about 20-25 minutes.

Egg Muffins

 10 mn

  25 mn

  12

1. Preheat your oven to 375°F and generously grease a 12-cup muffin tin with oil or use silicone muffin liners for easy removal. In a large bowl, whisk together the eggs, milk, salt, and pepper until well combined. Stir in the spinach, bell peppers, cooked bacon or sausage, and shredded cheese, along with any other mix-ins you're using. Mix well to ensure the ingredients are evenly distributed.

2. Pour the egg mixture into the prepared muffin cups, filling each about three-quarters full.

3. Bake in the preheated oven for 20-25 minutes, or until the egg muffins are set and lightly golden on top. Let the muffins cool in the pan for a few minutes before removing them. Serve warm.

4. Leftover muffins can be stored in an airtight container in the refrigerator for up to 4 days or frozen for longer storage. Reheat in the microwave or oven before serving

- 10 large eggs
- ½ cup milk
- Salt and pepper, to taste
- 1 cup spinach, finely chopped
- ½ cup bell peppers, diced
- ½ cup cooked and crumbled bacon or sausage
- ½ cup shredded cheese (optional)
- Additional mix-ins: mushrooms, onions, tomatoes, or feta cheese

 (per muffin): Calories: 120, Protein: 10g, Carbohydrates: 2g, Fat: 8g, Fiber: 0.5g, Sugar: 1g

 For the fluffiest muffins, avoid overmixing the egg mixture once you've added the milk. If you're making these ahead of time for meal prep, let the muffins cool completely before storing them to prevent sogginess.

Oat Pancakes with Blueberries

10 mn

15 mn

4

1. In a large mixing bowl, whisk together the oat flour, baking powder, and salt. In another bowl, mix the maple syrup, almond milk, beaten egg, melted coconut oil, and vanilla extract.

2. Gently fold the wet ingredients into the dry ingredients. Do this step with care. We aim for a smooth batter, but a few lumps are perfectly fine. Gently fold in the blueberries, distributing them evenly throughout the batter.

3. Heat a non-stick pan or griddle over medium heat and brush with a little coconut oil. Pour ¼ cup of batter for each pancake and cook until bubbles form on the surface, about 2-3 minutes. Flip and cook for an additional 1-2 minutes or until golden brown and cooked through.

4. Serve these golden beauties warm with a drizzle of maple syrup and a dollop of butter if you like.

- 1 ½ cups GF oat flour
- 2 tsp. baking powder
- ½ tsp. salt
- 2 Tbsp. maple syrup (plus more for serving)
- 1 cup almond milk
- 1 large egg, beaten (room temperature)
- 2 Tbsp. melted coconut oil (plus more for the pan)
- 1 tsp. vanilla extract
- 1 cup fresh blueberries
- Optional: Butter, for serving

(per serving): Calories: 250, Protein: 6g, Carbohydrates: 38g, Fat: 9g, Fiber: 5g, Sugar: 10g

If the batter seems too thick, add a little more almond milk to reach the desired consistency.

Vegan Tofu Scramble

10 mn

20 mn

4

1. In a small bowl, mix the nutritional yeast, turmeric, garlic powder, onion powder, salt, and black pepper. Set aside. Heat olive oil in a large skillet over medium heat. Add the diced onion and bell pepper, sautéing until softened and slightly caramelized, about 5-7 minutes.

2. Add the crumbled tofu to the skillet. Sprinkle the seasoning mix over the tofu and vegetables. Stir well to ensure the tofu is evenly coated with the spices. Cook for 5-10 minutes, or until the tofu is heated through and has absorbed the flavors.

3. Stir in the chopped spinach and diced tomato, cooking just until the spinach has wilted and the tomatoes are warmed through, about 2-3 minutes. Taste and adjust seasoning as needed. Remove from heat. Serve the tofu scramble hot, either on its own or accompanied by optional ingredients.

- 1 block (14 oz) firm tofu, drained and crumbled
- 2 Tbsp. nutritional yeast
- 1 tsp. turmeric powder
- ½ tsp. garlic powder
- ½ tsp. onion powder
- Salt and black pepper, to taste
- 2 Tbsp. olive oil
- 1 small onion, diced
- 1 bell pepper, diced
- 1 cup spinach, roughly chopped
- 1 tomato, diced
- Optional: avocado slices, gluten-free tortillas, or gluten-free bread for serving

(per serving): Calories: 200, Protein: 12g, Carbohydrates: 10g, Fat: 14g, Fiber: 3g, Sugar: 3g

For added depth of flavor, consider incorporating a splash of gluten-free soy sauce or tamari while cooking the tofu. Feel free to add other vegetables such as mushrooms, zucchini, or kale, depending on your preference or what you have on hand.

Chia Pudding

1. In a mixing bowl or mason jar, combine the chia seeds, almond milk, maple syrup or honey, and vanilla extract. Stir well to ensure the chia seeds are evenly distributed.
2. Cover and refrigerate the mixture for at least 2 hours, or overnight. This resting time allows the chia seeds to absorb the liquid and thicken into a pudding-like consistency.
3. Once set, give the pudding a good stir to break up any clumps. If the pudding is too thick, you can add a little more milk and stir until you reach your desired consistency.
4. Serve the chia pudding in bowls or glasses, topped with your choice toppings. Enjoy immediately, or cover and store in the refrigerator for up to 5 days.

5 mn*

0 mn

2

*plus at least 2 hours for setting

- ¼ cup chia seeds
- 1 cup almond milk
- 1 Tbsp. maple syrup or honey (adjust to taste)
- ½ tsp. vanilla extract
- Optional toppings: Fresh berries, sliced bananas, nuts or coconut flakes

(per serving): Calories: 180, Protein: 5g, Carbohydrates: 24g, Fat: 9g, Fiber: 10g Sugar: 8g

For a chocolate version, add 1 tablespoon of cocoa powder to the mixture before refrigerating.

Breakfast Salad with Avocado and Eggs

1. Poach or boil the eggs according to your preference. For poached eggs, bring a pot of water to a simmer, add a splash of vinegar, and gently drop in the eggs. Cook for about 3-4 minutes for runny yolks or longer for firmer yolks. For boiled eggs, place them in boiling water for 7-9 minutes, then cool in ice water and peel. In a small bowl, whisk together the olive oil and lemon juice. Season with salt and pepper to taste.
2. In a large bowl, toss the mixed greens, cherry tomatoes, cucumber, and red onion with the dressing until everything is lightly coated. Divide the dressed salad among plates. Top each with sliced avocado and an egg. Sprinkle with any optional toppings. Serve immediately.

15 mn

5 mn

4

- 4 cups mixed greens (spinach, arugula, kale, etc.)
- 2 ripe avocados, sliced
- 4 eggs, poached or boiled
- 1 cup cherry tomatoes, halved
- ½ cucumber, sliced
- ¼ red onion, thinly sliced
- 2 Tbsp. olive oil
- 1 Tbsp. lemon juice
- Salt and pepper, to taste
- Optional toppings: crumbled feta cheese, nuts, seeds, or gluten-free croutons

(per serving): Calories: 300, Protein: 10g, Carbohydrates: 14g, Fat: 24g, Fiber: 7g, Sugar: 3g

Experiment with the base greens to suit your taste; baby kale offers a tender texture, while arugula adds a peppery bite.

Lunch

- 2 large sweet potatoes, sliced into 1/2-inch thick rounds
- 3 Tbsp. olive oil
- 2 cloves garlic, minced
- 1 tsp. fresh rosemary, finely chopped
- 1/2 tsp. chili flakes (adjust to taste)
- Salt and pepper, to taste
- 1 cup grated mozzarella cheese
- Fresh parsley, for garnish

 (per serving): Calories: 250, Protein: 8g, Carbohydrates: 24g, Fat: 14g, Fiber: 3g, Sugar: 5g

Sweet Potato Melts with Rosemary, Garlic, and Chili

🧑‍🍳 10 mn

🍲 25 mn

🍴 5

1. Preheat your oven to 425°F. Line a baking sheet with parchment paper.
2. In a large bowl, toss the sweet potato rounds with olive oil, minced garlic, rosemary, chili flakes, salt, and pepper until evenly coated. Arrange the sweet potato rounds in a single layer on the prepared baking sheet. Roast in the preheated oven for 20 minutes, or until they are tender and starting to brown.
3. Remove the baking sheet from the oven and sprinkle the grated mozzarella cheese over each sweet potato round. Return to the oven and broil for 2-3 minutes, or until the cheese is melted and bubbly. Garnish with fresh parsley before serving.

For a crispier texture, flip the sweet potato rounds halfway through the roasting time before adding cheese. This dish can be customized with additional toppings before adding cheese, such as sliced olives, chopped bacon, or a dollop of sour cream.

- 8 eggs
- 1/2 cup milk (any kind)
- 1 cup fresh spinach, roughly chopped
- 1 cup cherry tomatoes, halved
- 1 small onion, finely diced
- 2 cloves garlic, minced
- 1/4 cup feta cheese, crumbled (optional)
- 2 Tbsp. olive oil
- Salt and pepper, to taste
- Fresh herbs for garnish (such as parsley or basil)

 (per serving): Calories: 300, Protein: 20g, Carbohydrates: 8g, Fat: 22g, Fiber: 2g, Sugar: 4g

Spinach and Tomato Frittata

🧑‍🍳 10 mn

🍲 25 mn

🍴 4

1. Preheat the oven to 375°F. In a medium bowl, whisk together the eggs, milk, salt, and pepper until well combined. Heat olive oil in an oven-safe skillet over medium heat. Add the onion and garlic, sautéing until the onion is translucent, about 5 minutes.
2. Add the spinach and cook until it's just wilted, about 2 minutes. Scatter the cherry tomatoes and feta cheese (if using) evenly over the spinach.
3. Pour the egg mixture into the skillet, making sure the eggs cover the vegetables evenly. Cook without stirring for about 2-3 minutes, until the edges begin to set. Transfer the skillet to the oven and bake for 15-20 minutes, or until the frittata is set and lightly golden on top.
4. Remove from the oven and let it cool for a few minutes. Garnish with fresh herbs before slicing and serving.

 Add other vegetables you have on hand, such as bell peppers, mushrooms, or zucchini, for a more filling and nutritious frittata. The frittata can be served hot, at room temperature, or even cold.

Beet and Goat Cheese Arugula Salad with Quinoa Cakes

1. In a large bowl, combine the arugula, sliced beets, crumbled goat cheese, and toasted walnuts. In a small bowl, whisk together balsamic vinegar and 2 Tbsp. of olive oil. Season with salt and pepper to taste. Dress the salad with the vinaigrette just before serving to keep the arugula crisp.

2. In a mixing bowl, combine the cooked quinoa, beaten egg, gluten-free flour, green onions, salt, and pepper. Mix well until the mixture is cohesive. Form the mixture into small patties.

3. Heat a generous amount of olive oil in a skillet over medium heat. Fry the quinoa cakes for 3-4 minutes on each side, or until they are golden and crispy. Remove from the skillet and drain on paper towels. Divide the dressed salad among plates. Top each with a few slices of beet and a couple of quinoa cakes. Sprinkle additional crumbled goat cheese and walnuts over the top if desired.

20 mn*

30 mn

4

*excluding beet roasting time

- 4 medium beets, roasted, peeled, and sliced
- 4 cups arugula
- 1/2 cup goat cheese, crumbled
- 1/4 cup walnuts, toasted and chopped
- 2 Tbsp. balsamic vinegar
- 4 Tbsp. olive oil, divided
- Salt and pepper, to taste

For the Crispy Quinoa Cakes
- 2 cups cooked quinoa (cooled)
- 1 egg, beaten
- 1/4 cup gluten-free flour
- 2 Tbsp. green onions, chopped
- Salt and pepper, to taste
- Olive oil, for frying

 (per serving): Calories: 400, Protein: 14g, Carbohydrates: 38g, Fat: 22g, Fiber: 6g Sugar: 9g

 For added flavor and color, mix golden and red beets. The quinoa cakes can be made in advance and reheated in the oven for a quick assembly.

Buckwheat and Roasted Vegetable Salad

1. Preheat the oven to 400°F. In a large mixing bowl, toss the zucchini, bell peppers, and red onion with 2 Tbsp. of olive oil, salt, and pepper until evenly coated. Spread the vegetables on a baking sheet in a single layer. Roast for 20-25 minutes, or until tender and lightly caramelized, stirring halfway through.

2. While the vegetables are roasting, bring 2 cups of water to a boil in a medium saucepan. Add the rinsed buckwheat groats, reduce heat to low, cover, and simmer for 10-12 minutes, or until the water is absorbed and the buckwheat is tender. Remove from heat and let it sit, covered, for 5 minutes. Fluff with a fork and allow to cool slightly.

3. Prepare the dressing by whisking together the balsamic vinegar, extra virgin olive oil, honey, Dijon mustard, salt, and pepper in a small bowl.

4. In a large salad bowl, combine the cooked buckwheat, roasted vegetables, chopped parsley, and crumbled feta cheese. Drizzle with the dressing and toss gently to combine.

5. Taste and adjust the seasoning with additional salt and pepper if needed. Serve warm or at room temperature.

15 mn

30 mn

4

- 1 cup buckwheat groats, rinsed
- 2 cups water
- 1 medium zucchini, cut into bite-sized pieces
- 1 red bell pepper, cut into bite-sized pieces
- 1 yellow bell pepper, cut into bite-sized pieces
- 1 red onion, cut into wedges
- 2 Tbsp. olive oil
- Salt and pepper, to taste
- 1/4 cup fresh parsley, chopped
- 1/4 cup feta cheese, crumbled
- 2 Tbsp. balsamic vinegar
- 2 Tbsp. extra virgin olive oil
- 1 tsp. honey (or maple syrup)
- 1 tsp. Dijon mustard
- Salt and pepper, to taste

 (per serving): Calories: 350, Protein: 9g, Carbohydrates: 45g, Fat: 16g, Fiber: 6g, Sugar: 8g

 Feel free to experiment with other vegetables like eggplant, cherry tomatoes, or butternut squash for different flavors and textures. Buckwheat groats can be cooked in vegetable broth instead of water for added flavor.

Roasted Cauliflower and Chickpea Wraps with a Tahini Dressing (Gluten-Free Tortillas)

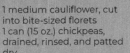

15mn

30 mn

4

1. Preheat the oven to 400°F. On a baking sheet, toss the cauliflower and chickpeas with olive oil, cumin, chili powder, garlic powder, salt, and pepper. Spread in an even layer and roast for 25-30 minutes, or until the cauliflower is tender and golden.

2. In a small bowl, whisk together tahini, lemon juice, minced garlic, and water. Start with 2 Tbsp. of water and add more as needed to achieve a creamy, pourable consistency. Season with salt and pepper to taste. Heat the gluten-free tortillas according to package instructions until they are soft and pliable.

3. Lay out the tortillas on a clean surface. On each tortilla, layer the mixed greens, a portion of the roasted cauliflower and chickpeas, and sliced red onion. Drizzle with the tahini dressing and add any optional toppings. Carefully roll up the tortillas, folding in the sides to enclose the filling. Serve immediately, with extra tahini dressing on the side for dipping if desired.

- 1 medium cauliflower, cut into bite-sized florets
- 1 can (15 oz.) chickpeas, drained, rinsed, and patted dry
- 2 Tbsp. olive oil
- 1 tsp. ground cumin
- 1/2 tsp. chili powder
- 1/2 tsp. garlic powder
- Salt and pepper, to taste
- Gluten-free tortillas
- 2 cups mixed greens (spinach, arugula, or kale)
- 1 small red onion, thinly sliced

For the Tahini Dressing
- 1/4 cup tahini
- 2 Tbsp. lemon juice
- 1 garlic clove, minced
- 2-4 Tbsp. water (as needed for consistency)
- Salt and pepper, to taste

Optional Toppings
- Sliced avocado
- Sliced cucumbers
- Fresh cilantro or parsley

 (per serving): Calories: 350, Protein: 12g, Carbohydrates: 45g, Fat: 16g, Fiber: 11g, Sugar: 8g

 Roasting the cauliflower and chickpeas brings out their natural sweetness and adds a delightful crunch. The tahini dressing can be prepared ahead of time and stored in the refrigerator. It may thicken upon chilling; simply stir in a little water to thin it before use.

Greek Salad

10 mn

0 mn

4

1. In a large salad bowl, combine the tomato wedges, cucumber slices, red onion slices, and Kalamata olives. Sprinkle the crumbled feta cheese over the top of the salad.

2. In a small bowl or jar, whisk together the extra virgin olive oil, red wine vinegar, dried oregano, salt, and pepper to create the dressing. Drizzle the dressing over the salad, tossing gently to ensure all the ingredients are well coated. Garnish with chopped fresh parsley before serving.

- 3 large ripe tomatoes, cut into wedges
- 1 cucumber, sliced into half-moons
- 1 red onion, thinly sliced
- 1/2 cup Kalamata olives, pitted
- 1 cup feta cheese, crumbled
- 1/4 cup extra virgin olive oil
- 2 Tbsp. red wine vinegar
- 1 tsp. dried oregano
- Salt and pepper, to taste
- Fresh parsley, chopped, for garnish

 (per serving): Calories: 250, Protein: 7g, Carbohydrates: 10g, Fat: 21g, Fiber: 2g, Sugar: 6g

 For the best flavor, use ripe, in-season tomatoes and high-quality extra virgin olive oil. For a more substantial meal, add chopped grilled chicken or slices of grilled pita bread on the side.

Teriyaki Chicken with Rice

1. Heat olive oil in a large skillet over medium heat. Add the chicken pieces and cook until they are golden brown and cooked through, about 5-7 minutes.

2. While the chicken is cooking, prepare the teriyaki sauce. In a small saucepan, combine tamari (or gluten-free soy sauce), water, honey (or maple syrup), rice vinegar, minced garlic, and grated ginger. Bring to a simmer over medium heat. Stir the cornstarch slurry into the saucepan. Continue cooking, stirring constantly, until the sauce thickens, about 2-3 minutes.

3. Once the chicken is cooked, pour the teriyaki sauce over it, making sure the chicken pieces are well coated with the sauce. Cook together for another 2 minutes to allow the flavors to meld.

4. Serve the teriyaki chicken over the cooked rice, garnished with sesame seeds and sliced green onions.

15 mn

20 mn

4

- 1 lb. chicken breast, cut into bite-sized pieces
- 1 Tbsp. olive oil
- 1 cup rice (preferably a short-grain variety), cooked

For the Gluten-Free Teriyaki Sauce
- 1/2 cup tamari or gluten-free soy sauce
- 1/4 cup water
- 2 Tbsp. honey or maple syrup
- 1 Tbsp. rice vinegar
- 1 clove garlic, minced
- 1 tsp. ginger, grated
- 1 Tbsp. cornstarch mixed with 2 Tbsp. water to form a slurry

 **(per serving):** Calories: 400, Protein: 28g, Carbohydrates: 50g, Fat: 9g, Fiber: 1g Sugar: 9g

 For an added vegetable component, stir-fry some bell peppers, broccoli, or snap peas in the skillet before adding the chicken. If you prefer a spicier dish, add a dash of chili flakes to the teriyaki sauce for some heat.

Caramelized Onion, Mushroom, and Goat Cheese Galette

1. In a large bowl, combine gluten-free flour and salt. Add cold, diced butter and use a pastry cutter or your fingers to blend into the flour until the mixture resembles coarse crumbs. Gradually add ice water, 1 tablespoon at a time, mixing until the dough comes together. Form into a disk, wrap in plastic, and refrigerate for at least 1 hour.

2. In a large skillet, heat olive oil over medium heat. Add the onions with a pinch of salt, and cook slowly, stirring occasionally, until they are deep golden brown and caramelized, about 20-25 minutes. Remove from the skillet and set aside.

3. In the same skillet, add a bit more olive oil if needed, and sauté the mushrooms until they are soft and all the moisture has evaporated. Stir in the thyme, salt, and pepper. Set aside to cool.

4. Preheat the oven to 375°F. On a piece of parchment paper, roll out the chilled dough into a 12-inch circle. Transfer the parchment and dough onto a baking sheet.

5. Spread the caramelized onions and cooked mushrooms over the dough, leaving a 2-inch border. Crumble the goat cheese over the top. Fold the edges of the dough over the filling, pleating as needed. Brush the crust with beaten egg. Bake for 35-40 minutes, or until the crust is golden and the filling is bubbly. Let cool slightly before serving.

90 mn*

40 mn

4-6

*including chilling time

Gluten-Free Crust
- 1 1/4 cups GF all-purpose flour
- 1/2 tsp. salt
- 1/2 cup cold butter, diced
- 4-6 Tbsp. ice water

Filling Ingredients
- 2 Tbsp. olive oil
- 2 large onions, thinly sliced
- 2 cups mushrooms, sliced (any variety)
- 1 tsp. fresh thyme leaves
- Salt and pepper, to taste
- 1/2 cup goat cheese, crumbled (ensure gluten-free)
- 1 egg, beaten (for egg wash)

 (per serving): Calories: 400, Protein: 10g, Carbohydrates: 35g, Fat: 25g, Fiber: 3g Sugar: 5g

 Ensure your butter and water are cold for the crust to achieve a flaky texture. Feel free to add spinach or kale to the filling for added nutrition.

· 1 1/2 cups Arborio rice
· 1 lb. mushrooms (such as cremini or button), thinly sliced
· 4 cups vegetable broth, kept warm
· 1 cup dry white wine (optional, can substitute with broth)
· 1 large onion, finely chopped
· 2 cloves garlic, minced
· 3 Tbsp. olive oil
· 1/2 cup Parmesan cheese, grated (ensure gluten-free)
· 2 Tbsp. fresh parsley, chopped
· Salt and pepper, to taste

 (per serving): Calories: 450, Protein: 15g, Carbohydrates: 65g, Fat: 13g, Fiber: 3g, Sugar: 3g

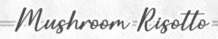
Mushroom Risotto

10 mn

30 mn

4

1. In a large skillet over medium heat, heat 2 tablespoons of olive oil. Add the mushrooms and cook until they are soft and browned, about 5-7 minutes. Remove the mushrooms from the skillet and set aside. In the same skillet, add the remaining tablespoon of olive oil and the onion. Sauté until the onion is translucent, about 5 minutes.

2. Add the garlic and Arborio rice to the skillet, stirring constantly for about 2 minutes or until the rice starts to slightly toast and become fragrant. If using wine, pour it into the skillet now, stirring continuously until the wine is mostly absorbed by the rice.

3. Begin adding the warm vegetable broth, one ladle at a time, stirring often. Wait until the liquid is almost fully absorbed before adding the next ladle of broth. Continue this process until the rice is tender yet firm to the bite, and the mixture is creamy, which should take about 18-20 minutes.

4. Stir the cooked mushrooms, Parmesan cheese, and parsley into the risotto. Season with salt and pepper to taste. Serve warm, garnishing with additional Parmesan and parsley if desired.

For an even more intense mushroom flavor, consider adding a few Tbsp. of porcini mushroom powder or rehydrated dried mushrooms to the risotto. Remember, the key to a perfect risotto is patience and constant stirring, ensuring each addition of broth is absorbed before adding the next.

*plus roasting time

· 4 medium beets, scrubbed, tops trimmed
· 6 cups mixed greens (such as spinach, arugula, and romaine)
· 1/2 cup goat cheese, crumbled
· 1/2 cup walnuts, toasted and roughly chopped
· 2 Tbsp. olive oil, plus extra for roasting beets
· Salt and pepper, to taste

For the Honey-Balsamic Dressing
· 1/4 cup balsamic vinegar
· 1/4 cup olive oil
· 2 Tbsp. honey
· 1 tsp. Dijon mustard
· Salt and pepper, to taste

 (per serving): Calories: 350, Protein: 10g, Carbohydrates: 20g, Fat: 127g, Fiber: 5g, Sugar: 15g

Roasted Beet, Goat Cheese, and Walnut Salad

15 mn*

15 mn

4

1. Preheat the oven to 400°F. Wrap the beets in aluminum foil with a drizzle of olive oil and a pinch of salt and pepper. Place on a baking sheet and roast in the preheated oven until tender, about 45-60 minutes. Once done, remove from the oven, let cool, then peel and cut into bite-sized pieces.

2. While the beets are cooling, prepare the honey-balsamic dressing. In a small bowl, whisk together balsamic vinegar, olive oil, honey, Dijon mustard, salt, and pepper until well combined. Adjust the seasoning as needed.

3. In a large salad bowl, toss the mixed greens with a portion of the dressing until lightly coated.

4. Add the roasted beets, goat cheese, and walnuts to the greens. Drizzle with the remaining dressing and gently toss to combine. Season with additional salt and pepper if desired, and serve immediately.

For a nuttier flavor, try using pecans or almonds in place of walnuts. This salad is versatile; feel free to add other elements like sliced oranges or strawberries for a fruity twist, or quinoa for a protein boost.

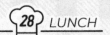

Turkey and Quinoa Meatballs

1. In a large bowl, combine the ground turkey, cooked quinoa, beaten egg, onion, garlic, parsley, salt, pepper, and smoked paprika. Mix until all ingredients are well incorporated.

2. Preheat your oven to 375°F. Line a baking sheet with parchment paper.

3. Form the mixture into meatballs, about the size of a golf ball, and place them on the prepared baking sheet. Drizzle the meatballs with olive oil, then bake in the preheated oven for 20-25 minutes, or until they are cooked through and golden on the outside.

4. While the meatballs are baking, warm the tomato sauce in a saucepan over medium heat. Serve the meatballs hot with the tomato sauce spooned over the top.

15 mn · 25 mn · 4

- 1 lb. ground turkey
- 1 cup cooked quinoa, cooled
- 1 egg, beaten
- 1/2 cup onion, finely chopped
- 2 cloves garlic, minced
- 1/4 cup parsley, chopped
- 1 tsp. salt
- 1/2 tsp. black pepper
- 1/2 tsp. smoked paprika
- 2 Tbsp. olive oil
- 1 cup tomato sauce

 (per serving): Calories: 300, Protein: 27g, Carbohydrates: 15g, Fat: 15g, Fiber: 2g Sugar: 3g

 These meatballs are versatile and can be served not only with tomato sauce but also in a sandwich, on top of a salad, or as part of a pasta dish with gluten-free pasta.

Butternut Squash and Sage Pasta

1. Preheat your oven to 425°F. Toss the cubed butternut squash with 2 tablespoons. of olive oil, salt, and pepper on a baking sheet. Spread into a single layer and roast in the preheated oven for 25-30 minutes, or until the squash is tender and begins to caramelize, stirring halfway through the cooking time.

2. While the squash is roasting, cook the pasta according to package instructions in a large pot of salted boiling water until al dente. Drain, reserving 1 cup of pasta water, and set aside.

3. Heat the remaining 1 tablespoon of olive oil in a large skillet over medium heat. Add the sage leaves and fry until crispy, about 1-2 minutes. Remove the sage with a slotted spoon and set aside on a paper towel. In the same skillet, add the minced garlic and sauté for about 1 minute, or until fragrant but not browned. Add the roasted butternut squash to the skillet with the garlic, tossing to combine. If the mixture seems dry, add a little of the reserved pasta water to create a light sauce.

4. Add the cooked pasta to the skillet, tossing everything together until the pasta is well coated with the sauce. If needed, add more pasta water to achieve your desired consistency.

5. Crumble the fried sage leaves over the pasta, and mix gently. Serve the pasta hot, garnished with grated Parmesan cheese and additional chopped sage.

15 mn · 35 mn · 4

- 1 medium butternut squash, peeled, seeded, and cut into 1/2-inch cubes
- 3 Tbsp. olive oil, divided
- Salt and pepper, to taste
- 10-12 fresh sage leaves
- 4 cloves garlic, minced
- 8 oz. GF pasta (such as penne, fusilli, or spaghetti)
- Grated Parmesan cheese, for serving
- Additional fresh sage, chopped, for garnish

 (per serving): Calories: 350, Protein: 8g, Carbohydrates: 50g, Fat: 14g, Fiber: 5g, Sugar: 4g

 For an extra flavor boost, roast the butternut squash with a sprinkle of nutmeg or cinnamon. This dish is best enjoyed fresh but can be refrigerated and gently reheated, adding a little water or olive oil to refresh the sauce.

Lemon Garlic Shrimp Pasta

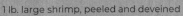

10 mn

20 mn

4

1. Cook the gluten-free pasta according to package instructions in a large pot of salted boiling water until al dente. Drain and set aside, reserving a cup of pasta water.

2. While the pasta is cooking, heat olive oil in a large skillet over medium heat. Add the garlic and chili flakes, sautéing for 1-2 minutes until fragrant but not browned.

3. Increase the heat to medium-high, add the shrimp to the skillet, and season with salt and pepper. Cook for 2-3 minutes on each side, or until the shrimp are pink and cooked through.

4. Stir in the lemon zest and lemon juice, tossing to combine. If the mixture seems dry, add a little of the reserved pasta water to loosen it up.

5. Add the cooked pasta to the skillet with the shrimp mixture. Toss everything together over low heat until the pasta is well coated with the sauce. If needed, add a bit more pasta water to achieve your desired sauce consistency. Remove from heat, stir in the chopped parsley, and adjust seasoning with additional salt, pepper, or lemon juice if needed. Serve immediately, garnished with lemon wedges on the side.

- 1 lb. large shrimp, peeled and deveined
- 8 oz. gluten-free spaghetti or linguine
- 3 Tbsp. olive oil
- 4 cloves garlic, minced
- 1/2 tsp red chili flakes (adjust to taste)
- Zest of 1 lemon
- Juice of 1 lemon
- 1/4 cup fresh parsley, chopped
- Salt and pepper, to taste
- Additional lemon wedges for serving

 (per serving): Calories: 400, Protein: 28g, Carbohydrates: 45g, Fat: 12g, Fiber: 2g, Sugar: 2g

 Ensure your shrimp are dry before cooking to get a good sear without steaming them. For an extra touch of flavor, add a splash of white wine to the skillet after cooking the shrimp, letting it reduce before adding the lemon juice and zest.

Curry Chicken with Basmati Rice

10 mn

35 mn

4

1. Heat olive oil in a large skillet over medium heat. Add the onion, garlic, and ginger, sautéing until the onion is translucent, about 5 minutes. Stir in the curry powder and cook for another minute, until fragrant. Add the chicken pieces to the skillet, seasoning with salt and pepper. Cook until the chicken is browned on all sides, about 5-7 minutes.

2. Pour in the coconut milk and diced tomatoes with their juice. Bring the mixture to a simmer, then reduce the heat to low and cover. Cook for 20-25 minutes, or until the chicken is tender and the sauce has thickened.

3. Taste and adjust seasoning with additional salt, pepper, or curry powder if needed. Serve the curry over cooked basmati rice, garnished with fresh cilantro.

- 1 lb. chicken breast, cut into bite-sized pieces
- 1 Tbsp. olive oil
- 1 large onion, finely chopped
- 2 cloves garlic, minced
- 1 Tbsp. ginger, grated
- 2 Tbsp. curry powder
- 1 can (14 oz.) coconut milk
- 1 can (14 oz.) diced tomatoes, undrained
- 1/2 tsp. salt
- 1/4 tsp. black pepper
- 2 cups basmati rice, cooked according to package instructions
- Fresh cilantro, for garnish

 (per serving): Calories: 550, Protein: 30g, Carbohydrates: 60g, Fat: 22g, Fiber: 2g, Sugar: 3g

For a richer flavor, you can substitute the chicken breast with chicken thighs. Adding vegetables like bell pepper, peas, or carrots can increase the dish's nutritional value and add color.

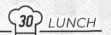

Spiralized Zucchini and Carrot Noodles with Peanut Sauce

15 mn

0 mn

4

1. Use a spiralizer to turn the zucchinis and carrots into noodles. Place them in a large bowl, along with the sliced red bell pepper, chopped cilantro, and sliced green onions.

2. In a small bowl, whisk together peanut butter, tamari (or gluten-free soy sauce), lime juice, honey (or maple syrup), minced garlic, and grated ginger until smooth. If the sauce is too thick, add warm water one tablespoon at a time until you reach the desired consistency. Add red pepper flakes or sriracha, if using, to taste.

3. Pour the peanut sauce over the spiralized vegetables in the bowl. Gently toss everything together until the noodles are evenly coated with the sauce.

4. Divide the noodles among plates and sprinkle with sesame seeds. Serve immediately.

- 2 large zucchinis, spiralized
- 2 large carrots, spiralized
- 1 red bell pepper, thinly sliced
- 1/4 cup cilantro, chopped
- 1/4 cup green onions, sliced
- 1 Tbsp. sesame seeds

For the Peanut Sauce
- 1/3 cup peanut butter (creamy or crunchy, based on preference)

- 2 Tbsp. tamari or gluten-free soy sauce
- 2 Tbsp. lime juice
- 1 Tbsp. honey or maple syrup
- 1 clove garlic, minced
- 1 tsp. ginger, grated
- 1-2 Tbsp. warm water (as needed to thin the sauce)
- Optional: Red pepper flakes or a dash of sriracha for heat

(per serving): Calories: 250, Protein: 8g, Carbohydrates: 24g, Fat: 15g, Fiber: 5g, Sugar: 10g

For extra protein, consider topping the noodles with grilled chicken, shrimp, or tofu. If you don't have a spiralizer, you can use a vegetable peeler to create thin strips of zucchini and carrot.

Lentil and Vegetable Soup

15 mn

40 mn

6

1. Heat olive oil in a large pot over medium heat. Add onion, carrots, and celery, and sauté until the vegetables begin to soften, about 5 minutes. Add garlic, cumin, thyme, and bay leaf, and cook for another minute until fragrant.

2. Stir in the lentils, diced tomatoes with their juice, vegetable broth, and water. Bring the mixture to a boil, then reduce the heat to low, cover, and simmer for about 25-30 minutes, or until the lentils are tender.

3. Once the lentils are cooked, add the chopped spinach and cook until the spinach is wilted, about 2 minutes. Remove from heat, discard the bay leaf, and stir in the lemon juice. Season with salt and pepper to taste. Serve hot, garnished with fresh parsley if desired.

- 1 cup dried lentils, rinsed
- 2 Tbsp. olive oil
- 1 large onion, diced
- 2 carrots, peeled and diced
- 2 stalks celery, diced
- 3 cloves garlic, minced
- 1 tsp. ground cumin
- 1/2 tsp. dried thyme
- 1 bay leaf
- 1 can (14.5 oz.) diced toma-

toes, with juice
- 6 cups vegetable broth
- 2 cups water
- 2 cups spinach leaves, roughly chopped
- Salt and pepper, to taste
- Juice of 1 lemon
- Optional: Fresh parsley for garnish

(per serving): Calories: 250, Protein: 12g, Carbohydrates: 38g, Fat: 5g, Fiber: 16g, Sugar: 6g

Soaking lentils overnight can reduce cooking time and make them easier to digest. This soup stores well in the refrigerator for up to 5 days or can be frozen for up to 3 months.

Black Bean and Quinoa Salad

20 mn

15 mn

4

- 1 cup quinoa, rinsed
- 2 cups water
- 1 can (15 oz.) black beans, rinsed and drained
- 1 red bell pepper, finely chopped
- 1 green bell pepper, finely chopped
- 1 cup corn kernels (fresh or thawed if frozen)
- 1 small red onion, finely diced
- ¼ cup fresh cilantro, chopped
- ¼ cup extra virgin olive oil
- 2 limes, juiced
- 1 tsp. ground cumin
- ½ tsp. salt
- ¼ tsp. black pepper
- 1 garlic clove, minced
- Optional toppings: diced avocado, crumbled feta cheese, or sliced jalapeños

(per serving): Calories: 320, Protein: 12g, Carbohydrates: 45g, Fat: 10g, Fiber: 10g, Sugar: 3g

1. In a medium saucepan, bring 2 cups of water to a boil. Add the rinsed quinoa, reduce the heat to low, cover, and simmer for about 15 minutes, or until all the water is absorbed. Remove from heat, let it sit covered for 5 minutes, then fluff with a fork and allow to cool.

2. In a small bowl, whisk together olive oil, lime juice, ground cumin, minced garlic, salt, and black pepper until well combined. In a large bowl, combine the cooled quinoa, black beans, red and green bell peppers, corn, red onion, and cilantro. Toss gently to mix.

3. Pour the vinaigrette over the salad and toss until everything is well coated. Adjust seasoning to taste.

4. Top with your favorite optional ingredients. For the best flavor, let the salad chill in the refrigerator for at least 30 minutes before serving.

Rinsing quinoa before cooking removes its natural bitterness. The salad can be customized with a variety of vegetables, beans, or grains according to your preference.

Grilled Fish Tacos

15 mn

10 mn

4*

*2 tacos each

- 1 lb. white fish fillets (such as cod, tilapia, or mahi-mahi)
- 2 Tbsp. olive oil
- 1 Tbsp. lime juice
- 1 tsp. chili powder
- 1/2 tsp. cumin
- 1/2 tsp. smoked paprika
- Salt and pepper, to taste
- 8 small gluten-free corn tortillas
- 2 cups cabbage, thinly sliced

- 1 avocado, sliced
- 1/4 cup fresh cilantro, chopped

For the Lime Crema
- 1/2 cup sour cream (ensure gluten-free)
- 2 Tbsp. lime juice
- 1 Tbsp. lime zest
- Salt, to taste

(per serving): Calories: 350, Protein: 25g, Carbohydrates: 35g, Fat: 15g, Fiber: 5g, Sugar: 3g

1. Preheat grill to medium-high heat. In a small bowl, whisk together olive oil, lime juice, chili powder, cumin, smoked paprika, salt, and pepper. Brush this mixture over both sides of the fish fillets.

2. Place fish on the grill and cook for 4-5 minutes per side or until the fish flakes easily with a fork. Remove from grill and let rest. While the fish is resting, warm the gluten-free corn tortillas on the grill for about 30 seconds on each side.

3. In a small bowl, mix together the sour cream, lime juice, lime zest, and salt to make the lime crema.

4. Flake the grilled fish into pieces. Assemble the tacos by placing some of the grilled fish onto each tortilla. Top with sliced cabbage, avocado, and cilantro. Drizzle with lime crema and serve immediately.

These tacos are also great with additional toppings like diced tomatoes, sliced radishes, or pickled onions. You can make a dairy-free lime crema using cashew cream or coconut yogurt as the base instead of sour cream.

Healthy Bean Salad

15 mn

0 mn*

6

1. In a large salad bowl, combine the black beans, kidney beans, chickpeas, red bell pepper, green bell pepper, red onion, corn, and cilantro. In a small bowl or jar, whisk together the olive oil, lime juice, red wine vinegar, honey, minced garlic, cumin, salt, and pepper to create the dressing.

2. Pour the dressing over the salad and toss gently to ensure all the ingredients are well coated.

3. Let the salad sit for at least 30 minutes in the refrigerator before serving to allow the flavors to meld together. Serve chilled or at room temperature.

*plus chilling time

- 1 can (15 oz.) black beans, rinsed and drained
- 1 can (15 oz.) kidney beans, rinsed and drained
- 1 can (15 oz.) chickpeas, rinsed and drained
- 1 red bell pepper, diced
- 1 green bell pepper, diced
- 1/2 red onion, finely chopped
- 1 cup fresh corn kernels (or thawed if frozen)
- 1/4 cup fresh cilantro, chopped

For the Dressing
- 1/4 cup olive oil
- 2 Tbsp. lime juice
- 1 Tbsp. red wine vinegar
- 1 tsp. honey (or maple syrup for a vegan option)
- 1 garlic clove, minced
- 1/2 tsp. cumin
- Salt and pepper, to taste

(per serving): Calories: 300, Protein: 10g, Carbohydrates: 45g, Fat: 9g, Fiber: 12g Sugar: 5g

Feel free to add other vegetables or herbs such as diced tomatoes, avocado, or parsley, for additional flavors and textures. For an extra protein boost, add quinoa or diced grilled chicken.

California Burger Wraps

15 mn

15 mn

4

1. Season the ground turkey or beef with salt and pepper. Form into 4 patties.

2. Cook the patties in a skillet over medium heat, or grill them, for about 5-7 minutes on each side or until fully cooked through. The internal temperature should reach 165°F for turkey and 160°F for beef.

3. While the patties are cooking, prepare the yogurt sauce (if using) by mixing the Greek yogurt, lemon juice, garlic, salt, and pepper in a small bowl. Set aside.

4. To assemble the wraps, place a lettuce leaf on a plate. On each lettuce leaf, place a cooked burger patty. Top each patty with slices of avocado, tomato, and red onion. Sprinkle shredded cheddar cheese over the top. Add a dollop of mustard, ketchup, or a spoonful of the yogurt sauce if desired.

5. Carefully fold the lettuce around the fillings to create a wrap. Serve immediately.

- 1 lb. ground turkey or lean ground beef
- 1 avocado, sliced
- 1 tomato, sliced
- 1/2 red onion, thinly sliced
- 4 large lettuce leaves (such as Bibb or iceberg), whole
- 1/4 cup shredded cheddar cheese
- Salt and pepper, to taste

- Optional toppings: mustard, ketchup, or a simple yogurt sauce

For the Simple Yogurt Sauce (Optional)
- 1/2 cup plain Greek yogurt
- 1 Tbsp. lemon juice
- 1 clove garlic, minced
- Salt and pepper, to taste

(per serving, without optional source): Calories: 350, Protein: 28g, Carbohydrates: 6g, Fat: 24g, Fiber: 3g, Sugar: 2g

The California Burger Wraps can be customized with additional toppings like bacon, pickles, or any other favorite burger toppings. Using large, sturdy lettuce leaves is key for a good wrap that holds together well.

Dinner

20 mn

45 mn

4

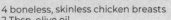

- 4 boneless, skinless chicken breasts
- 2 Tbsp. olive oil
- 2 lemons, one juiced and one sliced
- 3 cloves garlic, minced
- 1 Tbsp. fresh rosemary, chopped (or 1 teaspoon dried)
- Salt and pepper, to taste
- 1/4 cup GF chicken broth
- Additional rosemary sprigs and lemon slices for garnish

(per serving): Calories: 215, Protein: 25g, Carbohydrates: 3g, Fat: 12g, Fiber: 0g, Sugar: 1g

Lemon and Rosemary Chicken

1. Preheat your oven to 375°F. In a small bowl, combine olive oil, lemon juice, minced garlic, chopped rosemary, salt, and pepper. Place chicken breasts in a baking dish. Rub the marinade over and under the skin of the chicken, ensuring it's well coated. Arrange lemon slices around and on top of the chicken.

2. Pour the chicken broth around the chicken pieces in the baking dish. This helps keep the chicken moist while it cooks. Bake in the preheated oven for 35-45 minutes, or until the chicken is cooked through and the juices run clear. The internal temperature should reach 165°F.

3. Halfway through the cooking time, baste the chicken with the juices collected at the bottom of the baking dish. Once done, let the chicken rest for a few minutes before serving. Garnish with fresh rosemary sprigs and lemon slices.

 To infuse more flavor, marinate the chicken in the lemon and rosemary mixture for at least 1 hour or overnight in the refrigerator. If using bone-in, skin-on chicken pieces, adjust cooking times accordingly, as they may take longer to cook.

10 mn

15 mn

4

- 4 salmon fillets (about 6 oz. each)
- Salt and pepper, to taste
- 1 Tbsp. olive oil
- 1/4 cup honey
- 2 Tbsp. mustard
- 1 Tbsp. lemon juice
- 1 clove garlic, minced
- 1 tsp. fresh dill, chopped (or 1/2 teaspoon dried)

(per serving): Calories: 345, Protein: 23g, Carbohydrates: 18g, Fat: 19g, Fiber: 0g, Sugar: 17g

Baked Salmon with Honey Mustard Sauce

1. Preheat your oven to 400°F. Season the salmon fillets with salt and pepper. Place them skin-side down in a baking dish. Drizzle with olive oil.

2. In a small bowl, whisk together honey, mustard, lemon juice, garlic, and dill to create the sauce.

3. Generously brush the honey mustard sauce over the salmon fillets.

4. Bake in the preheated oven for 12-15 minutes, or until the salmon flakes easily with a fork. The cooking time may vary depending on the thickness of the fillets. Once done, remove from the oven and let it rest for a couple of minutes.

 If you prefer a thinner sauce, add a little water or extra lemon juice to adjust the consistency before brushing it onto the salmon.

Grilled Eggplant Rolls

20 mn

10 mn

4

1. Preheat your grill to medium-high heat. Season the eggplant slices with salt and pepper. Brush both sides of the slices with olive oil. Grill the eggplant slices for about 2-3 minutes on each side, or until tender and grill marks appear.

2. In a mixing bowl, combine ricotta cheese, basil, garlic, spinach, and sun-dried tomatoes. Mix well.

3. Lay the grilled eggplant slices flat on a working surface. Place a tablespoon of the ricotta mixture on one end of each slice. Roll up the slices tightly and secure with a toothpick if necessary.

4. Arrange the rolls on a serving platter. Sprinkle with grated Parmesan cheese before serving.

· 2 large eggplants, sliced lengthwise into 1/4 inch thick slices
· Salt and pepper, to taste
· 2 Tbsp. olive oil
· 1 cup ricotta cheese
· 1/4 cup fresh basil, chopped
· 1 clove garlic, minced
· 1 cup spinach, chopped
· 1/2 cup sun-dried tomatoes, chopped
· 1/4 cup Parmesan cheese, grated

 (per serving): Calories: 220, Protein: 9g, Carbohydrates: 15g, Fat: 14g, Fiber: 5g Sugar: 9g

 Enhance the flavor by adding a drizzle of balsamic glaze over the rolls before serving. If you don't have a grill, you can broil the eggplant slices in the oven until tender.

Pork Tenderloin with a Cherry Balsamic Reduction

15 mn

25 mn

4

1. Preheat your oven to 375°F. Season the pork tenderloin with salt and pepper.

2. Heat olive oil in a large oven-proof skillet over medium-high heat. Add the pork and sear on all sides until golden brown, about 2-3 minutes per side.

3. Transfer the skillet to the oven and roast the pork for 15-20 minutes, or until the internal temperature reaches 145°F. Remove from the oven and let it rest for 5 minutes.

4. While the pork is resting, prepare the cherry balsamic reduction. In a small saucepan, combine cherries, balsamic vinegar, honey, garlic, and thyme. Bring to a simmer over medium heat and cook until the sauce has thickened and reduced by half, about 10 minutes. Stir in the butter, if using, until melted and incorporated. Slice the pork tenderloin and drizzle with the cherry balsamic reduction before serving.

· 1 pork tenderloin (about 1 lb.)
· Salt and pepper, to taste
· 2 Tbsp. olive oil
· 1/2 cup cherries, pitted and halved (fresh or frozen)
· 1/4 cup balsamic vinegar
· 2 Tbsp. honey
· 1 clove garlic, minced
· 1 tsp. fresh thyme, chopped (or 1/2 teaspoon dried)
· 1 Tbsp. unsalted butter (optional, for richness)

(per serving): Calories: 310, Protein: 24g, Carbohydrates: 15g, Fat: 16g, Fiber: 1g, Sugar: 13g

To ensure even cooking, let the pork tenderloin sit at room temperature for about 20 minutes before cooking. For a more robust flavor, consider adding a splash of red wine to the reduction.

15mn

45 mn

6

Smoky Lentil Stew with Chorizo and Kale

1. Heat olive oil in a large pot over medium heat. Add the chorizo and cook until browned, about 5 minutes. Remove the chorizo from the pot and set aside.

2. In the same pot, add the onion, carrots, and celery. Cook until the vegetables are softened, about 5 minutes. Add the garlic and smoked paprika, cooking for another minute until fragrant.

3. Add the lentils, broth, and bay leaf to the pot. Season with salt and pepper. Bring to a boil, then reduce heat to low and simmer, covered, for 30 minutes, or until the lentils are tender.

4. Return the chorizo to the pot. Add the kale and simmer for another 10 minutes, or until the kale is wilted and the stew is heated through. Stir in the lemon juice, and adjust seasoning with more salt and pepper if needed. Remove the bay leaf before serving.

- 1 Tbsp. olive oil
- 1/2 lb. chorizo sausage, sliced
- 1 onion, chopped
- 2 carrots, peeled and diced
- 2 celery stalks, diced
- 3 cloves garlic, minced
- 1 tsp. smoked paprika
- 1 cup lentils (brown or green), rinsed
- 4 cups GF chicken or vegetable broth
- 1 bay leaf
- Salt and pepper, to taste
- 2 cups kale, stems removed and leaves chopped
- 1 Tbsp. lemon juice

(per serving): Calories: 290, Protein: 19g, Carbohydrates: 24g, Fat: 13g, Fiber: 9g, Sugar: 4g

Serve with a slice of gluten-free bread for a hearty and complete meal. Adding a splash of vinegar or a dollop of yogurt upon serving can enhance the flavors with a tangy note.

15 mn

5 mn

4

Grilled Shrimp with Garlic Sauce

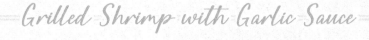

1. In a large bowl, combine the shrimp with 1 tablespoon of olive oil, salt, and pepper. Toss to coat evenly. Preheat your grill to medium-high heat.

2. Grill the shrimp for 2-3 minutes on each side, or until they are pink and slightly charred.

3. While the shrimp are grilling, prepare the garlic sauce. In a small skillet over medium heat, add the remaining olive oil and minced garlic. Cook until the garlic is fragrant but not browned, about 1-2 minutes. Remove from heat and stir in the chopped parsley, lemon juice, and red pepper flakes if using. Once the shrimp are done, toss them in the garlic sauce until well coated. Serve immediately, garnished with lemon wedges on the side.

- 1 lb. large shrimp, peeled and deveined
- 2 Tbsp. olive oil
- Salt and pepper, to taste
- 3 cloves garlic, minced
- 1/4 cup fresh parsley, chopped
- 1 Tbsp. lemon juice
- 1 tsp. red pepper flakes (optional for heat)
- Additional lemon wedges for serving

(per serving): Calories: 200, Protein: 24g, Carbohydrates: 2g, Fat: 10g, Fiber: 0g, Sugar: 0g

To ensure even cooking, avoid overcrowding the shrimp on the grill. Cook in batches if necessary. For an extra flavor boost, marinate the shrimp in the garlic sauce for 30 minutes to an hour before grilling.

Ginger Lime Chicken with Coconut Rice

1. In a mixing bowl, whisk together olive oil, lime juice, soy sauce, honey, ginger, garlic, salt, and pepper. Place the chicken breasts in a large ziplock bag or a shallow dish. Pour the marinade over the chicken, ensuring each piece is well coated. Seal or cover, and refrigerate for at least 2 hours, or overnight for best results.

2. Preheat your grill or grill pan to medium-high heat. Remove the chicken from the marinade, letting any excess drip off.

3. Grill the chicken for 6-8 minutes on each side, or until fully cooked through and charred on the outside. The internal temperature should reach 165°F. Rinse the jasmine rice under cold water until the water runs clear. In a medium saucepan, combine rinsed rice, coconut milk, water, sugar, and salt. Bring to a boil.

4. Once boiling, reduce the heat to low, cover, and simmer for 18-20 minutes, or until the liquid is absorbed and the rice is tender. Remove from heat and let it sit, covered, for 5 minutes. Fluff with a fork before serving.

30 mn*

30 mn

4

*plus marinating time

For the Ginger Lime Chicken:
4 boneless, skinless chicken breasts
1/4 cup olive oil
1/4 cup lime juice
2 Tbsp. soy sauce (ensure gluten-free)
2 Tbsp. honey
1 Tbsp. fresh ginger, grated

2 cloves garlic, minced
Salt and pepper, to taste

For the Coconut Rice:
1 cup jasmine rice
1 1/2 cups coconut milk
1/2 cup water
1 Tbsp. sugar
1/2 tsp. salt

 (per serving): Calories: 600, Protein: 28g, Carbohydrates: 58g, Fat: 28g, Fiber: 1g Sugar: 10g

 Marinating the chicken overnight will infuse it with more flavor and tenderness. For an added burst of flavor, garnish the coconut rice with toasted shredded coconut or chopped cilantro before serving.

Sweet Potato and Red Pepper Soup

1. Heat the olive oil in a large pot over medium heat. Add the onion and garlic, cooking until soft and translucent, about 5 minutes.

2. Add the sweet potatoes and red bell peppers to the pot, stirring to combine with the onion and garlic. Cook for an additional 5 minutes.

3. Pour in the vegetable broth, and season with salt, pepper, smoked paprika, and cayenne pepper if using. Bring to a boil, then reduce the heat to low and simmer for 20 minutes, or until the sweet potatoes are tender. Use an immersion blender to puree the soup until smooth. Alternatively, you can blend the soup in batches using a regular blender. Be careful of the hot liquid!

4. Taste and adjust seasoning as needed. Serve hot, garnished with a drizzle of fresh cream or coconut milk and a sprinkle of fresh cilantro or parsley.

15 mn

30 mn

4

2 Tbsp. olive oil
1 onion, chopped
2 cloves garlic, minced
2 large sweet potatoes, peeled and cubed
2 red bell peppers, deseeded and chopped
4 cups vegetable broth
Salt and pepper, to taste
1 tsp. smoked paprika
1/2 tsp. cayenne pepper (optional for heat)
Fresh cream or coconut milk for garnish (optional)
Fresh cilantro or parsley for garnish

 (per serving): Calories: 200, Protein: 3g, Carbohydrates: 35g, Fat: 6g, Fiber: 5g, Sugar: 12g

 Roasting the sweet potatoes and red peppers before adding them to the soup can enhance their flavors. Simply toss them with olive oil and roast in a 400°F oven for 20-25 minutes before proceeding with the recipe.

20 mn*

15 mn

4

*plus marinating time

For the Fajita Marinade:
- 1/4 cup lime juice
- 2 Tbsp. olive oil
- 2 cloves garlic, minced
- 1 tsp. cumin
- 1 tsp. smoked paprika
- 1/2 tsp. chili powder
- Salt and pepper, to taste

For the Fajitas:
- 1 lb. beef skirt steak
- 1 red bell pepper, sliced
- 1 green bell pepper, sliced
- 1 yellow bell pepper, sliced
- 1 onion, sliced
- Additional olive oil for cooking
- GF tortillas, for serving

1. In a small bowl, whisk together the lime juice, olive oil, garlic, cumin, smoked paprika, chili powder, salt, and pepper to make the marinade. Place the beef skirt steak in a large ziplock bag or shallow dish. Pour the marinade over the steak, ensuring it's well coated. Seal or cover and refrigerate for at least 2 hours, or overnight for best results.

2. Preheat a large skillet or grill pan over medium-high heat. Add a splash of olive oil. Remove the steak from the marinade, letting any excess drip off, and cook for 5-7 minutes on each side for medium-rare, or until done to your liking. Let it rest for a few minutes before slicing against the grain into thin strips.

3. In the same skillet, add a bit more olive oil if needed, and sauté the bell peppers and onion until they are soft and slightly charred, about 5-7 minutes.

4. Warm the gluten-free tortillas according to package instructions.

5. Assemble the fajitas by placing some of the beef strips and sautéed vegetables on each tortilla. Add any desired garnishes such as avocado slices, lime wedges, fresh cilantro, sour cream, and grated cheese. Serve immediately and enjoy.

 (per serving): Calories: 330, Protein: 26g, Carbohydrates: 12g, Fat: 20g, Fiber: 2g, Sugar: 4g

 For an authentic touch, char the tortillas on an open flame or in a dry skillet for a few seconds on each side. Vegetarians can substitute portobello mushrooms for the beef to enjoy a delicious plant-based version of this dish.

Chickpea and Spinach Curry

10 mn

20mn

4

- 2 Tbsp. olive oil
- 1 onion, finely chopped
- 2 cloves garlic, minced
- 1 Tbsp. fresh ginger, grated
- 1 Tbsp. curry powder
- 1 tsp. ground cumin
- 1 tsp. turmeric
- 1 can (14 oz) chickpeas, drained and rinsed
- 1 can (14 oz) diced tomatoes
- 1 can (14 oz) coconut milk
- 4 cups fresh spinach leaves
- Salt and pepper, to taste
- Fresh cilantro, chopped, for garnish
- Cooked rice or gluten-free naan, for serving

1. Heat the olive oil in a large skillet over medium heat. Add the onion and cook until soft and translucent, about 5 minutes. Add the garlic and ginger, and cook for another 1-2 minutes, until fragrant. Stir in the curry powder, cumin, and turmeric, cooking for another minute until the spices are well combined and aromatic.

2. Add the chickpeas, diced tomatoes (with their juice), and coconut milk to the skillet. Stir to combine all the ingredients. Bring the mixture to a simmer, then reduce the heat to low. Cook for 15 minutes, stirring occasionally.

3. Add the spinach to the skillet, and cook until wilted, about 2-3 minutes. Season with salt and pepper to taste. Serve the curry warm, garnished with chopped cilantro. Accompany with cooked rice or gluten-free naan as desired.

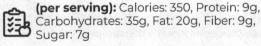 **(per serving):** Calories: 350, Protein: 9g, Carbohydrates: 35g, Fat: 20g, Fiber: 9g, Sugar: 7g

 For a thicker curry, mash some of the chickpeas with the back of a spoon before adding the spinach. This dish is versatile; feel free to add other vegetables such as bell peppers or sweet potatoes for extra nutrition and flavor.

Vegan Buddha Bowl

20 mn

30 mn

4

1. Preheat your oven to 400°F. In a medium saucepan, combine quinoa and water. Bring to a boil, then reduce heat to low, cover, and simmer for 15-20 minutes, or until all the water is absorbed. Remove from heat and let it sit covered for 5 minutes. Fluff with a fork and set aside.

2. Toss chickpeas with 1 tablespoon of olive oil, smoked paprika, garlic powder, salt, and pepper. Spread on a baking sheet and bake for 20-25 minutes, until crispy. Toss sweet potatoes with the remaining olive oil, salt, and pepper. Spread on a separate baking sheet and bake for 25-30 minutes, until tender. In a large skillet over medium heat, sauté kale until wilted, about 3-5 minutes. Season with a pinch of salt.

3. Prepare the dressing by whisking together tahini, lemon juice, maple syrup, water, and salt until smooth. Adjust the consistency with more water if necessary.

4. Assemble the Buddha bowls by dividing the cooked quinoa among four bowls. Top with roasted chickpeas, sweet potatoes, sautéed kale, avocado slices, red bell pepper, cucumber, and carrot.

5. Drizzle each bowl with the tahini dressing before serving.

For the Bowl:
- 2 cups quinoa, rinsed
- 4 cups water
- 1 can (15 oz) chickpeas, drained, rinsed, and patted dry
- 1 tsp. smoked paprika
- 1 tsp. garlic powder
- Salt and pepper, to taste
- 2 Tbsp. olive oil, divided
- 2 sweet potatoes, peeled and cubed
- 2 cups kale, stems removed and chopped
- 1 avocado, sliced
- 1 red bell pepper, sliced
- 1 cucumber, sliced
- 1 carrot, julienned or shredded

For the Dressing:
- 1/4 cup tahini
- 2 Tbsp. lemon juice
- 1 Tbsp. maple syrup
- 2-4 Tbsp. water, to adjust consistency
- Salt, to taste

 (per serving): Calories:600, Protein: 18g, Carbohydrates: 80g, Fat: 25g, Fiber: 15g Sugar: 10g

 Feel free to customize your Buddha bowl with any seasonal vegetables or your favorite toppings. Roasted broccoli, beets, or butternut squash are excellent additions. For an extra protein boost, consider adding baked tofu or tempeh to the bowl.

Hunter's Chicken

20 mn

40 mn

4

1. Season the chicken breasts with salt and pepper. Heat olive oil in a large skillet over medium-high heat. Add the chicken and cook until browned on both sides, about 3-4 minutes per side. Remove the chicken from the skillet and set aside.

2. In the same skillet, add the onion, garlic, red bell pepper, and mushrooms. Sauté until the vegetables are softened, about 5 minutes. Stir in the diced tomatoes, chicken broth, tomato paste, oregano, and basil. Bring the mixture to a simmer.

3. Return the chicken to the skillet, nestling it into the sauce. Cover and simmer for 25-30 minutes, or until the chicken is cooked through. Garnish with fresh parsley before serving.

- 4 boneless, skinless chicken breasts
- Salt and pepper, to taste
- 2 Tbsp. olive oil
- 1 onion, finely chopped
- 2 cloves garlic, minced
- 1 red bell pepper, sliced
- 1 cup mushrooms, sliced
- 1 can (14 oz) diced tomatoes, undrained
- 1/2 cup chicken broth (ensure gluten-free)
- 1 Tbsp. tomato paste
- 1 tsp. dried oregano
- 1 tsp. dried basil
- Fresh parsley, chopped, for garnish

 (per serving): Calories: 280, Protein: 27g, Carbohydrates: 14g, Fat: 12g, Fiber: 3g, Sugar: 7g

 For a richer flavor, you can add a splash of red wine to the sauce when adding the tomatoes. For a thicker sauce, you can add a tablespoon of gluten-free flour mixed with a bit of water to the skillet before returning the chicken to the pan.

Grilled Salmon with Lemon and Parsley Sauce

15 mn

10 mn

4

1. Preheat your grill to medium-high heat. Brush the salmon fillets with olive oil and season them with salt and pepper.
2. Grill the salmon, skin-side down, for about 5-6 minutes. Flip carefully and grill for another 3-4 minutes or until the salmon is just cooked through and easily flakes with a fork.
3. While the salmon is grilling, prepare the lemon and parsley sauce. In a small bowl, whisk together the parsley, olive oil, lemon juice, garlic, salt, and pepper until well combined.
4. Once the salmon is cooked, remove from the grill and place on a serving platter. Drizzle the lemon and parsley sauce over the top of the salmon. Garnish with lemon slices before serving.

For the Salmon:
- 4 salmon fillets (about 6 oz. each)
- 2 Tbsp. olive oil
- Salt and pepper, to taste
- Lemon slices, for garnish

For the Lemon and Parsley Sauce:
- 1/4 cup fresh parsley, finely chopped
- 1/4 cup olive oil
- 2 Tbsp. lemon juice
- 1 clove garlic, minced
- Salt and pepper, to taste

(per serving): Calories: 320, Protein: 23g, Carbohydrates: 1g, Fat: 25g, Fiber: 0g, Sugar: 0g

For an extra flavor boost, let the salmon marinate in a portion of the lemon and parsley sauce for 30 minutes to an hour before grilling.

Herb-Crusted Rack of Lamb with Root Vegetable Puree

30 mn

40 mn

4

1. Preheat your oven to 400°F. Season the racks of lamb with salt and pepper. Heat olive oil in a large skillet over medium-high heat. Sear the lamb for 2-3 minutes on each side until browned. Transfer to a baking dish.
2. In a bowl, mix together the garlic, parsley, rosemary, thyme, and breadcrumbs. Brush the racks of lamb with Dijon mustard, then press the herb breadcrumb mixture onto the mustard coating.
3. Roast in the preheated oven for 20-25 minutes for medium-rare, or until the desired doneness is reached. Let rest for 10 minutes before carving into chops.
4. Bring a large pot of salted water to a boil. Add the carrots, parsnip, and sweet potato. Boil until the vegetables are tender, about 20 minutes.
5. Drain the vegetables and transfer them to a food processor. Add the cream (or coconut milk) and butter (or olive oil), and puree until smooth. Season with salt and pepper to taste.

For the Herb-Crusted Rack of Lamb:
- 2 racks of lamb (about 1.5 lb.s each), trimmed
- Salt and pepper, to taste
- 2 Tbsp. olive oil
- 2 cloves garlic, minced
- 1/4 cup fresh parsley, finely chopped
- 2 Tbsp. fresh rosemary, finely chopped
- 2 Tbsp. fresh thyme, finely chopped
- 1/4 cup breadcrumbs (ensure gluten-free)
- 2 Tbsp. Dijon mustard

For the Root Vegetable Puree:
- 2 large carrots, peeled and cubed
- 1 large parsnip, peeled and cubed
- 1 small sweet potato, peeled and cubed
- 1/4 cup heavy cream or coconut milk
- 2 Tbsp. unsalted butter or olive oil
- Salt and pepper, to taste

(per serving): Calories: 750, Protein: 45g, Carbohydrates: 30g, Fat: 50g, Fiber: 5g, Sugar: 8g

For an extra crispy crust, broil the lamb for the last 2-3 minutes of cooking. The root vegetable puree can be made in advance and reheated, adding a little extra cream or butter if needed for smoothness.

Sweet and Spicy Pumpkin Chili

1. Heat the olive oil in a large pot over medium heat. Add the onion and garlic, cooking until softened, about 5 minutes. Increase the heat to medium-high and add the ground meat to the pot. Cook, breaking it apart with a spoon, until browned and cooked through.

2. Stir in the pumpkin puree, diced tomatoes, broth, black beans, kidney beans, chipotle peppers, chili powder, cumin, and smoked paprika. Season with salt and pepper to taste.

3. Bring the chili to a boil, then reduce the heat to low. Simmer, uncovered, for at least 45 minutes to an hour, stirring occasionally. The chili should thicken and flavors meld together.

4. Taste and adjust seasoning as needed. Serve hot, with optional garnishes of sour cream, shredded cheese, green onions, or cilantro on top.

20 mn

60 mn

6

- 2 Tbsp. olive oil
- 1 onion, diced
- 2 cloves garlic, minced
- 1 lb. ground beef or turkey
- 1 can (15 oz) pumpkin puree
- 1 can (14 oz) diced tomatoes, undrained
- 2 cups beef or vegetable broth
- 1 can (15 oz) black beans,
- drained and rinsed
- 1 can (15 oz) kidney beans, drained and rinsed
- 2 chipotle peppers in adobo sauce, finely chopped
- 1 tablespoon chili powder
- 1 teaspoon ground cumin
- 1 teaspoon smoked paprika
- Salt and pepper, to taste

 (per serving): Calories: 350, Protein: 25g, Carbohydrates: 30g, Fat: 15g, Fiber: 9g Sugar: 8g

 For a vegetarian version, omit the ground meat and add an extra can of beans or lentils. Adding a splash of apple cider vinegar or a squeeze of lime juice before serving can brighten the flavors.

Grilled Pepper Steak with Honey Onions

1. In a small bowl, whisk together olive oil, balsamic vinegar, soy sauce, black pepper, garlic powder, and onion powder. Place the steaks in a shallow dish or a resealable plastic bag. Pour the marinade over the steaks, ensuring they are well coated. Refrigerate and marinate for at least 2 hours, or overnight for best results. Preheat your grill to medium-high heat.

2. Remove the steaks from the marinade, letting the excess drip off. Season with salt to taste.

3. Grill the steaks to your desired doneness, about 4-6 minutes per side for medium-rare, depending on the thickness. Remove from the grill and let rest for 5 minutes.

4. While the steaks are resting, prepare the honey onions. Heat olive oil in a skillet over medium heat. Add the onions, honey, salt, and pepper. Cook, stirring occasionally, until the onions are caramelized and golden brown, about 15 minutes. Serve the grilled steaks topped with the honey onions.

15 mn*

20 mn

4

*plus marinating time

- 4 beef steaks (such as sirloin or ribeye)
- 2 Tbsp. olive oil
- 2 Tbsp. balsamic vinegar
- 2 Tbsp. soy sauce (ensure gluten-free)
- 1 tablespoon black pepper, coarsely ground
- 2 teaspoons garlic powder
- 1 teaspoon onion powder
- Salt, to taste

For the Honey Onions:
- 2 large onions, sliced
- 2 Tbsp. honey
- 1 tablespoon olive oil
- Salt and pepper, to taste

 (per serving): Calories: 550, Protein: 45g, Carbohydrates: 20g, Fat: 35g, Fiber: 2g, Sugar: 1g

 Allow the steaks to come to room temperature for about 20 minutes before grilling for more even cooking. The honey onions can also be prepared in advance and reheated before serving, making this dish even easier to put together for a quick meal.

20 mn

40mn

4

- 4 large bell peppers, halved and seeds removed
- 1 cup quinoa, rinsed
- 2 cups vegetable broth
- 1 Tbsp. olive oil
- 1 onion, diced
- 2 cloves garlic, minced
- 1 can (15 oz) black beans, drained and rinsed
- 1 cup corn kernels (fresh, frozen, or canned)
- 1 can (14 oz) diced tomatoes, drained
- 1 tsp. chili powder
- 1 tsp. cumin
- 1/2 tsp. smoked paprika
- Salt and pepper, to taste
- 1 cup shredded cheese

1. Preheat your oven to 375°F (190°C). Place the bell pepper halves in a baking dish, cut-side up.

2. In a medium saucepan, bring the vegetable broth to a boil. Add the quinoa, reduce heat to low, cover, and simmer for 15 minutes, or until the liquid is absorbed. Remove from heat and let it sit covered for 5 minutes. Fluff with a fork.

3. Heat the olive oil in a large skillet over medium heat. Add the onion and garlic, and sauté until softened, about 5 minutes. To the skillet, add the cooked quinoa, black beans, corn, diced tomatoes, chili powder, cumin, smoked paprika, salt, and pepper. Stir to combine and cook until the mixture is heated through, about 5 minutes.

4. Spoon the quinoa mixture into each bell pepper half, packing it tightly. Cover the baking dish with aluminum foil.

5. Bake in the preheated oven for about 25 minutes. Remove the foil, sprinkle the stuffed peppers with cheese, and bake for an additional 15 minutes, or until the cheese is melted and bubbly.

6. Serve the stuffed peppers with guacamole, sour cream, and fresh cilantro on the side, if desired.

(per serving): Calories: 400, Protein: 18g, Carbohydrates: 55g, Fat: 15g, Fiber: 12g, Sugar: 10g

Choose bell peppers that are similar in size to ensure even cooking. For added protein, consider incorporating ground meat or meat substitute into the quinoa mixture.

Chicken and Broccoli Pie

20 mn

30 mn

6

- 1 Tbsp. olive oil
- 1 onion, finely chopped
- 2 cloves garlic, minced
- 1 lb. chicken breast, cooked and shredded
- 2 cups broccoli florets, steamed and chopped
- 1 cup grated cheese
- 1/2 cup milk
- 4 eggs, beaten
- Salt and pepper, to taste
- 1 GF pie crust, prebaked according to package instructions

1. Preheat your oven to 375°F. Heat the olive oil in a skillet over medium heat. Add the onion and garlic, and sauté until softened, about 5 minutes.

2. In a large bowl, combine the sautéed onion and garlic, shredded chicken, chopped broccoli, half of the cheese, milk, eggs, salt, and pepper. Stir until well mixed.

3. Pour the chicken and broccoli mixture into the prebaked pie crust. Sprinkle the remaining cheese on top. Bake in the preheated oven for 30 minutes, or until the filling is set and the top is golden brown.

4. Let the pie cool for a few minutes before slicing and serving.

(per serving): Calories: 350, Protein: 25g, Carbohydrates: 15g, Fat: 20g, Fiber: 2g, Sugar: 3g

For a lower carb option, you can omit the pie crust and bake the filling in a greased pie dish as a crustless pie. Ensure all added vegetables are cooked to remove excess moisture before adding them to the pie filling to prevent a soggy crust.

Chicken Cordon Bleu

1. Preheat your oven to 350°F. Flatten the chicken breasts to about 1/4 inch thickness using a meat mallet or rolling pin. Season both sides with salt and pepper.

2. Place a slice of ham and a slice of cheese on each chicken breast, and roll them up tightly. Secure with toothpicks if necessary. Dip each chicken roll in beaten eggs, then coat with gluten-free breadcrumbs. Heat the olive oil and butter in a large oven-proof skillet over medium-high heat. Add the chicken rolls and cook until browned on all sides, about 5 minutes.

3. Transfer the skillet to the oven and bake for 20-25 minutes, or until the chicken is cooked through.

4. While the chicken is baking, in a small saucepan, combine the chicken broth, Dijon mustard, and lemon juice. Bring to a simmer and cook until slightly thickened, about 5 minutes.

5. Remove the chicken from the oven and let it rest for a few minutes before removing the toothpicks.

6. Serve the chicken cordon bleu sliced, drizzled with the mustard sauce.

 20 mn
 30 mn
 4

- 4 boneless, skinless chicken breasts
- Salt and pepper, to taste
- 4 slices of ham (ensure gluten-free)
- 4 slices of Swiss cheese
- 1 cup gluten-free breadcrumbs
- 2 eggs, beaten
- 2 Tbsp. olive oil
- 1 tablespoon butter
- 1/2 cup chicken broth (ensure gluten-free)
- 1 tablespoon Dijon mustard
- 1 teaspoon lemon juice

 (per serving): Calories: 400, Protein: 35g, Carbohydrates: 20g, Fat: 20g, Fiber: 1g Sugar: 2g

 Ensure the chicken rolls are tightly secured to keep the filling inside during cooking. For a crispy crust, you can briefly broil the chicken after baking, watching carefully to avoid burning.

Roasted Cauliflower Steaks with Hazelnut Gremolata

1. Preheat your oven to 425°F. Line a baking sheet with parchment paper. Remove the leaves from the cauliflower and trim the stem, ensuring the head sits flat. Slice the cauliflower vertically into 1-inch thick steaks. Depending on the size, you should get about 2-3 steaks per head.

2. Arrange the cauliflower steaks on the prepared baking sheet. Brush both sides of each steak with olive oil and season with salt and pepper. Roast in the preheated oven for about 20-25 minutes, or until the cauliflower is tender and golden brown, flipping halfway through cooking.

3. While the cauliflower is roasting, prepare the gremolata. In a small bowl, mix together the chopped hazelnuts, lemon zest, garlic, parsley, olive oil, and salt.

4. Once the cauliflower steaks are done, plate them and generously top with the hazelnut gremolata.

 15 mn
 25 mn
 4

For the Cauliflower Steaks:
- 2 large heads of cauliflower
- 3 Tbsp. olive oil
- Salt and pepper, to taste

For the Hazelnut Gremolata:
- 1/2 cup hazelnuts, toasted and roughly chopped
- Zest of 1 lemon
- 2 cloves garlic, minced
- 1/4 cup fresh parsley, finely chopped
- 2 Tbsp. olive oil
- Salt, to taste

 (per serving): Calories: 280, Protein: 6g, Carbohydrates: 15g, Fat: 23g, Fiber: 6g, Sugar: 5g

 To ensure the cauliflower steaks hold together, try to keep the stem intact when slicing. This dish can be served as a main course for a vegetarian meal or as a side dish to complement meat or fish.

Snacks & Appetizers

- 1 cup cooked quinoa
- 1 cup fresh spinach, finely chopped
- 1/2 cup grated Parmesan cheese
- 1/4 cup GF breadcrumbs
- 2 cloves garlic, minced
- 1 large egg
- 1 tsp. Italian seasoning
- Salt and pepper, to taste
- 1 Tbsp. olive oil, for cooking
- Marinara sauce, for serving (ensure it's gluten-free)

 (per serving, without sauce): Calories: 210, Protein: 10g, Carbohydrates: 25g, Fat: 8g, Fiber: 3g, Sugar: 2g

Quinoa and Spinach Meatballs

🕐 20 mn
🍲 25 mn
🍴 4

1. Preheat your oven to 375°F and line a baking sheet with parchment paper.
2. In a large bowl, combine the cooked quinoa, chopped spinach, grated Parmesan, gluten-free breadcrumbs, minced garlic, egg, Italian seasoning, salt, and pepper. Mix until the ingredients are well combined. Form the mixture into small bite-sized meatballs. If the mixture feels too wet, you can add a bit more breadcrumbs to help it hold together.
3. Heat the olive oil in a skillet over medium heat. Add the meatballs and cook until they're browned on all sides. This step adds flavor and helps the meatballs hold their shape.
4. Transfer the browned meatballs to the prepared baking sheet and bake in the preheated oven for 15 minutes, or until they're cooked through. Serve the quinoa and spinach meatballs hot, topped with marinara sauce.

 Experiment with adding other vegetables or herbs into the mix for different flavors. For a smoother texture, the spinach can be lightly sautéed before being added to the mixture, although this is optional.

*about 12 poppers
- 6 jalapeño peppers, halved lengthwise and seeds removed
- 4 oz. brie cheese, cut into slices to fit jalapeño halves
- 1/4 cup cranberry sauce
- 1/4 cup gluten-free breadcrumbs
- 1 Tbsp. olive oil
- Salt and pepper, to taste

 (per serving, 3 poppers): Calories: 200, Protein: 6g, Carbohydrates: 12g, Fat: 14g, Fiber: 1g, Sugar: 6g

Cranberry Brie Jalapeno Poppers

🕐 20 mn
🍲 15 mn
🍴 4*

1. Preheat your oven to 375°F. Line a baking sheet with parchment paper.
2. Arrange the jalapeño halves on the prepared baking sheet cut side up. If the jalapeños have trouble standing, you can slice a small portion off the bottom to create a flat surface.
3. Place a slice of brie cheese into each jalapeño half. Spoon a small amount of cranberry sauce over the brie. In a small bowl, mix the gluten-free breadcrumbs with the olive oil, salt and pepper until the breadcrumbs are evenly coated with the oil. Sprinkle the seasoned breadcrumbs over the cranberry sauce on each jalapeño half.
4. Bake in the preheated oven for 15 minutes, or until the breadcrumbs are golden and the cheese is melted and bubbly. Let the jalapeño poppers cool for a few minutes before serving.

For a smoother cranberry sauce topping, you can briefly process the cranberry sauce in a blender or food processor. For an added touch of freshness, garnish the poppers with a sprinkle of chopped fresh cilantro or parsley after baking.

Mini Eggplant Pizzas

1. Preheat your oven to 400°F (200°C). Line a baking sheet with parchment paper for easy cleanup.

2. Arrange the eggplant slices in a single layer on the baking sheet. Brush both sides of each slice with olive oil and season with salt and pepper.

3. Bake the eggplant slices for 10 minutes, then flip and bake for an additional 5 minutes. This pre-baking ensures the eggplants are partially cooked before adding the toppings.

4. Remove the eggplant slices from the oven. Top each slice with a spoonful of marinara sauce, spreading it to cover. Sprinkle shredded mozzarella cheese over the sauce and add cherry tomato halves. Return the eggplant pizzas to the oven and bake for another 5 minutes, or until the cheese is melted and bubbly.

5. Garnish the mini eggplant pizzas with fresh basil leaves and any other optional toppings you've chosen. Serve immediately.

10 mn

20 mn

4

- 2 medium eggplants, sliced into 1/2-inch thick rounds
- 1 Tbsp. olive oil
- Salt and pepper, to taste
- 1 cup marinara sauce (ensure it's gluten-free)
- 1 cup shredded mozzarella cheese
- 1/2 cup cherry tomatoes, halved
- 1/4 cup fresh basil leaves, torn
- Optional toppings: sliced olives, sautéed mushrooms, anchovies, or any other pizza topping

 (per serving, without optional toppings): Calories: 215, Protein: 10g, Carbohydrates: 18g, Fat: 12g, Fiber: 6g Sugar: 11g

 For extra crispy eggplant pizzas, consider broiling them for the last 1-2 minutes of cooking time. Eggplant slices release moisture as they cook, so it's best to consume these mini pizzas immediately for the best texture.

Kale Chips with Tahini

1. Preheat your oven to 350°F. Line a baking sheet with parchment paper. In a large bowl, toss the kale pieces with olive oil and a sprinkle of salt until evenly coated. Spread the kale in a single layer on the prepared baking sheet, ensuring the pieces do not overlap for even cooking.

2. Bake for 10-15 minutes, or until the edges are slightly browned and the kale is crispy. Keep a close eye on them, as they can quickly go from perfect to burnt.

3. While the kale chips are baking, prepare the tahini dressing. In a small bowl, whisk together the tahini, lemon juice, minced garlic, and water (add one tablespoon at a time until you reach your desired consistency). Season with salt and pepper to taste. Once the kale chips are done, let them cool slightly on the baking sheet. They will continue to crisp up as they cool. Serve the kale chips with the tahini dressing on the side for dipping or drizzle the dressing over the chips before serving.

10 mn

15 mn

4

- 1 large bunch of kale, stems removed and leaves torn into bite-sized pieces
- 2 Tbsp. olive oil
- Salt, to taste

For the Tahini Dressing:
- 1/4 cup tahini (sesame seed paste)
- 2 Tbsp. lemon juice
- 1 clove garlic, minced
- 2-4 Tbsp. water, as needed to thin
- Salt and pepper, to taste

 (per serving, without dressing): Calories: 138, Protein: 4g, Carbohydrates: 10g, Fat: 10g, Fiber: 2g, Sugar: 0g

 Make sure the kale is thoroughly dry after washing to prevent steaming instead of crisping in the oven.

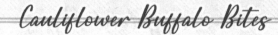

20 mn

25 mn

4

- 1 head cauliflower, cut into bite-sized florets
- 3/4 cup GF all-purpose flour
- 1 cup water
- 1/2 teaspoon garlic powder
- Salt and pepper, to taste
- 1 cup gluten-free buffalo sauce
- Dairy-free ranch or blue cheese dressing for serving

1. Preheat your oven to 450°F. Line a baking sheet with parchment paper for easy cleanup.

2. In a large bowl, whisk together the gluten-free flour, water, garlic powder, salt, and pepper until smooth to create your batter.

3. Dip each cauliflower floret into the batter, ensuring it's well coated. Gently shake off any excess batter and place the florets on the prepared baking sheet in a single layer.

4. Bake for 20 minutes, turning halfway through, until the florets are golden and starting to crisp.

5. While the cauliflower is baking, heat the buffalo sauce in a small pot over low heat or in the microwave until warmed through. Once the cauliflower is done, carefully toss the baked florets in the warmed buffalo sauce. Ensure each piece is well coated, then return them to the baking sheet.

6. Bake for an additional 5 minutes to set the sauce. Serve the cauliflower buffalo bites hot with dairy-free ranch or blue cheese dressing on the side. Celery and carrot sticks make great companions for a complete snacking experience.

(per serving, without dressing):
Calories: 198, Protein: 6g, Carbohydrates: 41g, Fat: 2g, Fiber: 5g, Sugar: 4g

For a crispier texture, you can increase the oven temperature slightly or broil the florets for a couple of minutes at the end of baking. Just keep a close eye on them to prevent burning.

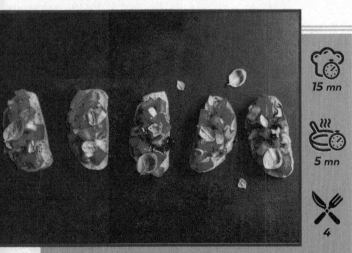

Tomato and Basil Bruschetta

15 mn

5 mn

4

- 4 large ripe tomatoes, finely diced
- 1/4 cup fresh basil leaves, chopped
- 2 cloves garlic, minced
- 1 Tbsp. extra virgin olive oil
- 1 tsp. balsamic vinegar
- Salt and pepper, to taste
- 1 GF baguette, sliced and toasted
- Optional: 1 garlic clove, halved, for rubbing on the toasted baguette slices

1. In a medium bowl, combine the diced tomatoes, chopped basil, minced garlic, extra virgin olive oil, and balsamic vinegar. Gently toss to ensure the ingredients are well mixed. Season with salt and pepper to taste. Let the mixture sit for about 10 minutes to allow the flavors to meld together.

2. While the tomato mixture is resting, toast the slices of gluten-free baguette. For added flavor, lightly rub one side of each toasted slice with the halved garlic clove.

3. Spoon a generous amount of the tomato mixture onto each toasted baguette slice. Make sure to include some of the juices, which are full of flavor. Serve immediately, while the baguette slices are still warm and crispy, to enjoy the contrast with the cool, fresh tomato topping.

(per serving, without optional garlic rub):
Calories: 180, Protein: 4g, Carbohydrates: 28g, Fat: 6g, Fiber: 3g, Sugar: 4g

For the best flavor, use tomatoes that are ripe and full of flavor. Different varieties of tomatoes can be mixed to enhance the taste and visual appeal of the bruschetta.

Sweet Potato Crostini with Avocado and Smoked Salmon

1. Preheat your oven to 400°F. Line a baking sheet with parchment paper for easy cleanup.
2. Toss the sweet potato rounds with olive oil and season with salt and pepper. Arrange them in a single layer on the prepared baking sheet. Bake for 20-25 minutes, flipping halfway through, until the sweet potatoes are tender and the edges start to crisp up.
3. Once the sweet potato rounds have cooled slightly, assemble the crostini. Place a slice of avocado on each sweet potato round, followed by a piece of smoked salmon.
4. Sprinkle the finely chopped red onion and capers over the top of each crostini. Garnish with fresh dill to add both flavor and a touch of color. If desired, serve the crostini with lemon wedges on the side.

 20 mn

 25 mn

 4

- 2 large sweet potatoes, sliced into 1/4-inch thick rounds
- 2 Tbsp. olive oil
- Salt and pepper, to taste
- 1 ripe avocado, thinly sliced
- 4 oz. smoked salmon, sliced into pieces
- 1/4 cup red onion, finely chopped
- 1 Tbsp. capers, drained
- Fresh dill for garnish
- Optional: lemon wedges for serving

 (per serving): Calories: 230, Protein: 10g, Carbohydrates: 18g, Fat: 14g, Fiber: 4g Sugar: 5g

 Sweet potatoes vary greatly in size. For uniform cooking, try to select sweet potatoes that are similar in size and cut the rounds as evenly as possible.

Vegetable Spring Rolls

1. Prepare all your vegetables and have them ready for assembly. Fill a large bowl with warm water for dipping the rice paper wrappers. Dip one rice paper wrapper at a time into the warm water for about 15-20 seconds until it's just soft and pliable. Lay it out on a clean, slightly damp cloth.
2. On the bottom third of the wrapper, arrange a small handful of lettuce, a few sticks of carrot, cucumber, and red bell pepper, a sprinkle of mint and cilantro leaves, and a few slices of avocado if using. Gently fold in the sides of the wrapper, then roll it up tightly from the bottom, enclosing the filling. Repeat with the remaining wrappers and filling.
3. For the dipping sauce, whisk together the peanut butter, tamari, lime juice, honey, and chili garlic sauce in a small bowl. Gradually add warm water until you achieve your desired consistency for dipping. Serve the spring rolls with the peanut dipping sauce on the side.

 30 mn

 0 mn

 4

- 8-10 rice paper wrappers
- 1 cup vermicelli rice noodles, cooked according to package instructions and cooled
- 1 cup lettuce, thinly sliced
- 1 cup carrot, julienned
- 1 cup cucumber, julienned
- 1/2 cup red bell pepper, julienned
- 1/2 cup fresh mint leaves
- 1/2 cup fresh cilantro leaves
- Optional: avocado slices, for added creaminess

For the Peanut Dipping Sauce:
- 1/4 cup natural peanut butter (ensure gluten-free)
- 2 Tbsp. tamari or gluten-free soy sauce
- 1 Tbsp. lime juice
- 1 Tbsp. honey or maple syrup
- 1 tsp. chili garlic sauce or to taste
- 2-4 Tbsp. warm water, to thin

 (per serving, without dipping sauce): Calories: 220, Protein: 4g, Carbohydrates: 41g, Fat: 4g, Fiber: 3g, Sugar: 6g

 Keep the rice paper wrappers covered with a damp towel after soaking to prevent them from drying out as you assemble the spring rolls. Feel free to customize the fillings based on your preference. Other great additions include thinly sliced avocado, bean sprouts, or tofu for added protein.

15 mn

25 mn

4

- 2 large sweet potatoes, thinly sliced into rounds
- 2 Tbsp. olive oil
- Salt and pepper, to taste
- 1 cup black beans, drained and rinsed
- 1 cup corn kernels (fresh, frozen and thawed, or canned and drained)
- 1 red bell pepper, diced
- 1/2 red onion, diced
- 1 cup shredded cheddar cheese
- 1 avocado, diced
- 1/4 cup fresh cilantro, chopped
- 1 lime, cut into wedges for serving

 (per serving): Calories: 380, Protein: 12g, Carbohydrates: 45g, Fat: 19g, Fiber: 9g, Sugar: 9g

1. Preheat your oven to 425°F (220°C). Line a large baking sheet with parchment paper.
2. Toss the sweet potato rounds with olive oil, salt, and pepper in a large bowl until evenly coated. Spread them in a single layer on the prepared baking sheet, ensuring they do not overlap too much.
3. Bake for 20-25 minutes, flipping halfway through, until the sweet potatoes are tender and the edges are starting to crisp up.
4. Remove the sweet potatoes from the oven. Sprinkle black beans, corn kernels, red bell pepper, and red onion over the sweet potatoes. Top with shredded cheese.
5. Return the baking sheet to the oven and bake for an additional 5 minutes, or until the cheese is melted and bubbly. Once out of the oven, top with diced avocado and fresh cilantro. Serve immediately with lime wedges on the side, and if desired, jalapeños, sour cream or a dairy-free alternative, and salsa.

 For extra crispiness, try not to overcrowd the sweet potato rounds on the baking sheet. They crisp up better when they have a little space around them.

20 mn*

10 mn

4

*plus marinating time
- 1 lb. large shrimp, peeled and deveined
- 2 cups pineapple, cut into 1-inch chunks
- 1/4 cup olive oil
- 2 Tbsp. soy sauce (ensure gluten-free)
- 1 Tbsp. honey
- 1 clove garlic, minced
- 1 tsp ginger, grated
- Salt and pepper, to taste
- 1 lime, juiced
- Fresh cilantro, for garnish

 (per serving): Calories: 260, Protein: 24g, Carbohydrates: 19g, Fat: 10g, Fiber: 1g, Sugar: 14g

1. In a bowl, whisk together the olive oil, gluten-free soy sauce, honey, minced garlic, grated ginger, salt, pepper, and lime juice to create the marinade. Add the shrimp to the marinade, ensuring they are well coated. Cover and let marinate in the refrigerator for at least 30 minutes, or up to 2 hours for more flavor. Preheat your grill to medium-high heat.
2. Thread the marinated shrimp and pineapple chunks alternately onto the skewers.
3. Grill the skewers for 2-3 minutes on each side, or until the shrimp are opaque and cooked through, and the pineapple is slightly caramelized. Garnish with fresh cilantro before serving. Serve hot, accompanied by extra lime wedges for squeezing over the top.

 Ensure the shrimp are not over-marinated, as the acidity from the lime juice can start to "cook" the shrimp. If using wooden skewers, soak them in water for at least 30 minutes to prevent burning.

Chicken and Zucchini Meatballs

1. Preheat your oven to 400°F and line a baking sheet with parchment paper.
2. In a large bowl, combine the ground chicken, grated zucchini, gluten-free breadcrumbs, Parmesan cheese, egg, minced garlic, Italian seasoning, salt, and pepper. Mix until well combined.
3. Shape the mixture into meatballs, about 1 to 1.5 inches in diameter, and place them on the prepared baking sheet. Brush each meatball lightly with olive oil. This helps to get a golden color and a slightly crispy outer layer. Bake in the preheated oven for 20-25 minutes, or until the meatballs are cooked through and lightly golden on the outside.
4. Serve the chicken and zucchini meatballs hot, topped with warm marinara sauce.

20 mn

25 mn

4

- 1 lb. ground chicken
- 1 cup zucchini, grated and excess moisture squeezed out
- 1/2 cup gluten-free breadcrumbs
- 1/4 cup Parmesan cheese, grated
- 1 egg
- 2 cloves garlic, minced
- 1 tsp. Italian seasoning
- Salt and pepper, to taste
- 2 Tbsp. olive oil, for baking
- Marinara sauce, for serving (ensure it's gluten-free)

 (per serving, without sauce):
Calories: 270, Protein: 27g, Carbohydrates: 8g, Fat: 14g, Fiber: 1g Sugar: 2g

 Squeezing the excess moisture out of the grated zucchini is crucial to prevent the meatballs from becoming too wet and falling apart. For added flavor, you can mix some chopped fresh herbs, such as parsley or basil, into the meatball mixture.

Baked Zucchini Chips

1. Preheat your oven to 425°F. Line a baking sheet with parchment paper.
2. In a large bowl, gently toss the thinly sliced zucchini with olive oil, ensuring each slice is lightly coated. Season with salt, pepper, and any optional seasonings you prefer.
3. Arrange the zucchini slices in a single layer on the prepared baking sheet, making sure they do not overlap. Bake in the preheated oven for 15-20 minutes, or until the zucchini slices are crispy and golden brown. Flip the slices halfway through the cooking time to ensure even crispiness.
4. Remove the chips from the oven and let them cool on the baking sheet for a few minutes. They will continue to crisp up as they cool.
5. Serve the baked zucchini chips immediately for the best texture.

15 mn

15 mn

4

- 2 large zucchinis, thinly sliced
- 2 Tbsp. olive oil
- Salt and pepper, to taste
- Optional seasonings: garlic powder, paprika, or Parmesan cheese

 (per serving, without optional seasoning):
Calories: 70, Protein: 1g, Carbohydrates: 45g, Fat: 6g, Fiber: 1g, Sugar: 3g

 The key to crispy zucchini chips is slicing the zucchini as thinly as possible. A mandoline slicer is ideal for getting uniform, thin slices. Pat the zucchini slices dry with paper towels before tossing them with olive oil to remove excess moisture. This step is crucial for achieving a crispy texture.

Avocado Lime Deviled Eggs

20 mn

10 mn

4*

1. Place the eggs in a saucepan and cover with water. Bring to a boil over high heat. Once boiling, cover the saucepan, turn off the heat, and let the eggs sit in the hot water for 10 minutes.

2. After 10 minutes, transfer the eggs to an ice water bath to cool quickly. This stops the cooking process and makes peeling easier.

3. Once cooled, peel the eggs and cut them in half lengthwise. Gently remove the yolks and place them in a medium bowl.

4. Add the ripe avocado and lime juice to the bowl with the egg yolks. Mash the mixture until smooth. Season with salt, pepper, and paprika.

5. Spoon or pipe the avocado and egg yolk mixture back into the egg whites.

6. Garnish with a sprinkle of paprika and optional chopped cilantro, diced tomatoes, or sliced jalapeños for an extra pop of color and flavor.

*8 halves
- 4 large eggs
- 1 ripe avocado
- 1 Tbsp. lime juice
- Salt and pepper, to taste
- 1/2 tsp. paprika, plus extra for garnish
- Optional garnishes: chopped cilantro, diced tomatoes, or sliced jalapeños

(per serving, 2 halves): Calories: 140, Protein: 6g, Carbohydrates: 5g, Fat: 11g, Fiber: 3g, Sugar: 1g

For a smoother filling, use a food processor to blend the egg yolks, avocado, and lime juice. This will create a creamy, uniform texture. If making ahead, add the lime juice to prevent the avocado from browning and cover tightly with plastic wrap, pressing it directly onto the surface of the filling before refrigerating.

Pear and Gorgonzola Crostini with Balsamic Reduction

15 mn

20 mn*

4

1. Begin by preparing the balsamic reduction. Pour the balsamic vinegar into a small saucepan and bring to a simmer over medium heat. Reduce the heat to low and let it simmer, stirring occasionally, until the vinegar has thickened and reduced to about 1/4 cup. This should take around 20 minutes. Set aside to cool; it will continue to thicken as it cools.

2. While the balsamic reduction is cooling, toast the slices of gluten-free baguette until they are lightly crisp. Arrange the toasted crostini on a serving platter. Place a few slices of pear on each piece of toasted baguette.

3. Sprinkle crumbled gorgonzola cheese over the pear slices. If you're using a dairy-free cheese alternative, ensure it has a similar texture and flavor profile to gorgonzola. Drizzle the cooled balsamic reduction over the pear and cheese-topped crostini. Garnish each crostini with fresh thyme leaves for an aromatic touch. Serve the Pear and Gorgonzola Crostini with Balsamic Reduction immediately.

*for balsamic reduction
- 1 cup balsamic vinegar
- 1 GF baguette, sliced and toasted
- 2 ripe pears, thinly sliced
- 1/2 cup crumbled gorgonzola cheese
- Fresh thyme leaves for garnish

(per serving): Calories: 280, Protein: 7g, Carbohydrates: 42g, Fat: 10g, Fiber: 3g, Sugar: 18g

The ripeness of the pears is crucial for this recipe. Choose pears that are ripe yet firm, which will provide a sweet flavor and a pleasant texture contrast to the creamy gorgonzola and the crisp crostini.

Roasted Chickpeas with Rosemary and Sea Salt

⏱ 5 mn

🍳 40 mn

🍴 4

1. Preheat your oven to 400°F. Line a baking sheet with parchment paper or a silicone baking mat for easy cleanup.

2. After draining and rinsing the chickpeas, pat them dry with paper towels or a clean kitchen towel. It's important to remove as much moisture as possible to ensure they become crispy when roasted.

3. In a mixing bowl, toss the dried chickpeas with olive oil, ensuring they are evenly coated.

4. Spread the chickpeas in a single layer on the prepared baking sheet. Roast in the preheated oven for 30-40 minutes, or until crispy and golden brown. Shake the pan or stir the chickpeas halfway through the roasting time to ensure even cooking.

5. Once roasted, immediately toss the chickpeas with the chopped rosemary and sea salt while they are still warm. Add black pepper if using. Let the chickpeas cool slightly before serving. They are best enjoyed warm but can also be stored in an airtight container once completely cooled.

- 2 cans (15 oz each) chickpeas, drained, rinsed, and thoroughly dried
- 2 Tbsp. olive oil
- 1 Tbsp. fresh rosemary, finely chopped
- 1 tsp. sea salt, or to taste
- Optional: 1/4 tsp. ground black pepper, or to taste

 (per serving): Calories: 215, Protein: 9g, Carbohydrates: 29g, Fat: 7g, Fiber: 8g Sugar: 5g

 For the crispiest chickpeas, make sure to dry them thoroughly after rinsing. Any residual moisture can steam the chickpeas in the oven, preventing them from getting crispy.

Caprese Bites

⏱ 15 mn

🍳 0 mn

🍴 4*

1. If using toothpicks or skewers, prepare them by laying them out on your work surface.

2. Assemble the caprese bites by skewering a cherry tomato, a basil leaf (fold it if large), and a mozzarella ball onto each toothpick or skewer. Arrange the assembled caprese bites on a serving platter. Drizzle the extra virgin olive oil and balsamic glaze evenly over the bites. The balsamic glaze adds a sweet and tangy flavor that complements the freshness of the tomato, basil, and mozzarella.

3. Season with salt and pepper to taste. The seasoning will enhance the natural flavors of the ingredients. Serve immediately, offering a burst of classic Italian flavors in every bite.

*about 16 bites
- 16 cherry tomatoes
- 16 small mozzarella balls (bocconcini), drained
- 16 fresh basil leaves
- 2 Tbsp. extra virgin olive oil
- 1 Tbsp. balsamic glaze
- Salt and pepper, to taste
- Optional: Toothpicks or small skewers for serving

 (per serving, 4 bites): Calories: 150, Protein: 8g, Carbohydrates: 3g, Fat: 12g, Fiber: 1g, Sugar: 2g

 For an extra touch of flavor, you can marinate the mozzarella balls in a mixture of olive oil, balsamic vinegar, salt, pepper, and some dried herbs like oregano or thyme before assembling the bites.

Beet Hummus

15 mn*

45 mn**

6

1. If you're starting with raw beets, preheat your oven to 400°F (200°C). Wrap the beets in aluminum foil and roast them on a baking sheet in the oven for about 45 minutes, or until tender. Once done, let them cool, then peel and cube.

2. In a food processor, combine the roasted beet cubes, chickpeas, minced garlic, tahini, lemon juice, and salt. Blend until smooth.

3. With the food processor running, gradually add the 2 Tbsp of olive oil and blend until the hummus reaches your desired consistency.

4. Taste and adjust the seasoning, adding more salt or lemon juice if needed.

5. To serve, transfer the hummus to a serving bowl. Create a swirl on the top with a spoon and drizzle with a bit more olive oil. Sprinkle sesame seeds and chopped parsley over the top for garnish, if desired. Adding a few additional beet cubes can enhance the visual appeal and add a burst of color.

6. Enjoy your beet hummus with gluten-free crackers, vegetable sticks, or as a vibrant spread on sandwiches.

excluding roasting time for beets
** *for roasting beets (if not using pre-cooked)*

- 2 medium-sized beets, roasted, peeled, and cubed
- 1 can (15 oz) chickpeas, drained and rinsed
- 2 cloves garlic, minced
- 2 Tbsp. tahini (sesame seed paste)
- 2 Tbsp. lemon juice
- Salt to taste
- 2 Tbsp. olive oil, plus more for drizzling

 (per serving): Calories: 168, Protein: 5g, Carbohydrates: 20g, Fat: 8g, Fiber: 5g, Sugar: 3g

 For a silkier hummus, peel the chickpeas by gently squeezing them to remove the skins. Experiment with adding other spices such as cumin or smoked paprika.

Greek Sushi

20 mn

0 mn

4

1. Carefully lay out the cucumber slices on a clean, flat surface. Pat them dry with a paper towel to remove any excess moisture. This will help the ingredients stick better.

2. Spread a thin layer of hummus over each cucumber slice.

3. On one end of each cucumber slice, arrange a small amount of feta cheese, kalamata olives, roasted red peppers, and spinach leaves. Starting from the end with the filling, carefully roll up the cucumber slices tightly, similar to how sushi rolls are made. Serve the Greek sushi immediately, accompanied by tzatziki sauce for dipping if desired.

- 1 cucumber, sliced into thin strips using a mandoline or a sharp knife
- 1/2 cup hummus (ensure gluten-free)
- 1/4 cup feta cheese, crumbled
- 1/4 cup kalamata olives, pitted and chopped
- 1/4 cup roasted red peppers, sliced into thin strips
- 1/4 cup spinach leaves, thinly sliced
- Optional: tzatziki sauce for dipping

 (per serving, without tzatziki sauce): Calories: 345, Protein: 23g, Carbohydrates: 18g, Fat: 19g, Fiber: 0g, Sugar: 17g

If you find the cucumber slices break when rolling, you can double up the slices for extra strength or let them sit out for a few minutes to become more pliable. Try adding different ingredients like chickpeas, artichoke hearts, or thinly sliced red onions.

Chipotle Cheese Crackers

1. Preheat your oven to 350°F and line a baking sheet with parchment paper.

2. In a large bowl, combine the almond flour, shredded cheddar cheese, nutritional yeast (if using), chipotle powder, garlic powder, and salt. Mix well to distribute the flavors evenly.

3. Add the egg to the dry ingredients. Mix until a dough forms. If the dough seems too dry, you can add a teaspoon of water at a time until it comes together. Place the dough between two sheets of parchment paper and roll out to about 1/8 inch thick. Remove the top sheet of parchment paper.

4. Using a pizza cutter or a sharp knife, cut the dough into small squares or desired shapes.

5. If using, sprinkle the tops of the crackers with sesame seeds or poppy seeds and lightly press them into the dough. Transfer the parchment paper with the cut dough onto the prepared baking sheet.

6. Bake in the preheated oven for 12-15 minutes, or until the edges of the crackers begin to brown slightly. Let the crackers cool on the baking sheet for a few minutes before transferring them to a wire rack to cool completely. They will continue to crisp up as they cool.

15 mn · **15 mn** · **6**

- 1 cup almond flour
- 1 cup shredded sharp cheddar cheese
- 1 Tbsp. nutritional yeast (for added cheesy flavor, optional)
- 1 tsp. chipotle powder
- 1/2 tsp. garlic powder
- 1/4 tsp. salt
- 1 egg
- Optional: sesame seeds or poppy seeds for topping

 (per serving): Calories: 220, Protein: 10g, Carbohydrates: 6g, Fat: 18g, Fiber: 3g Sugar: 1g

 The key to crisp crackers is rolling the dough evenly. Thicker areas will bake more slowly, resulting in unevenly cooked crackers.

Queso Fundido

1. Preheat your oven to 375°F if you plan to bake the queso fundido for a bubbly top, or you can also prepare it on the stovetop for a quicker version.

2. Heat the olive oil in a medium skillet over medium heat. Add the crumbled chorizo and cook until it starts to brown, about 5 minutes. Use a slotted spoon to remove the chorizo, leaving the fat in the pan. In the same skillet with the chorizo fat, add the chopped onion and jalapeño pepper. Sauté until the onion is translucent and the jalapeño is soft, about 5 minutes.

3. If baking, transfer the onion and jalapeño mixture to a baking dish. Add the diced tomato and cooked chorizo, mixing slightly. Top evenly with the shredded cheese.

4. Bake in the preheated oven until the cheese is melted and bubbly, about 10 minutes. Alternatively, you can cover the skillet (if oven-proof) with a lid and let the cheese melt over low heat on the stovetop. Garnish with chopped cilantro before serving. Serve warm with gluten-free tortilla chips for dipping.

10 mn · **15 mn** · **4**

- 1 Tbsp. olive oil
- 1/2 lb. chorizo (ensure gluten-free), casing removed and crumbled
- 1 small onion, finely chopped
- 1 jalapeño pepper, seeded and finely chopped
- 1 tomato, seeded and diced
- 2 cups shredded mozzarella cheese
- 1/4 cup cilantro, chopped (for garnish)
- Gluten-free tortilla chips, for serving

 (per serving, wothout tortilla chips): Calories: 390, Protein: 24g, Carbohydrates: 6g, Fat: 31g, Fiber: 1g, Sugar: 3g

For a lighter version, you can substitute the chorizo with ground turkey or chicken seasoned with a blend of paprika, garlic powder, cumin, and a touch of cayenne for heat. Adding a splash of beer or tequila to the chorizo and vegetable mixture can deepen the flavors. Just allow the alcohol to cook off before proceeding with the recipe.

Desserts

*plus chilling time

- 2 cups unsweetened almond milk
- 1/4 cup granulated sweetener of choice
- 1/4 cup unsweetened cocoa powder
- 2 Tbsp. cornstarch (ensure gluten-free)
- 1/4 tsp. salt
- 1 tsp. vanilla extract

 (per serving): Calories: 90, Protein: 2g, Carbohydrates: 12g, Fat: 4g, Fiber: 3g, Sugar: 1g

Low-Sugar Chocolate Pudding

🧁 10 mn

🍲 10 mn*

🍴 4

1. In a medium saucepan, whisk together the almond milk, granulated sweetener, cocoa powder, cornstarch, and salt until smooth and well combined.

2. Place the saucepan over medium heat and cook, whisking constantly, until the mixture starts to thicken and just begins to bubble, about 5-7 minutes. Be careful not to let it boil vigorously to prevent the pudding from becoming lumpy. Once the mixture has thickened to the consistency of a soft pudding, remove from heat and stir in the vanilla extract.

3. Divide the pudding into serving dishes or a large bowl. To prevent a skin from forming on top, place plastic wrap directly on the surface of the pudding. Chill in the refrigerator for at least 2 hours, or until set. Before serving, you can whisk the pudding again for a smoother texture, if desired.

For a creamier pudding, consider blending the chilled pudding in a blender until smooth and creamy. This can help achieve a silky texture. Garnish with a light sprinkle of sea salt, fresh berries, or a dollop of whipped coconut cream for added flavor and presentation.

Chocolate Banana Cupcakes

🧁 20 mn

🍲 18 mn

🍴 12

1. Preheat your oven to 350°F. Line a muffin tin with paper or silicone cupcake liners.

2. In a large bowl, whisk together the gluten-free flour, cocoa powder, baking soda, and salt. In another bowl, mix the granulated sugar, vegetable oil, and mashed banana until well combined. Stir in the water and vanilla extract.

3. Gradually add the wet ingredients to the dry ingredients, mixing until just combined. Be careful not to overmix. Fold in the vinegar, then gently stir in the chocolate chips.

4. Divide the batter evenly among the prepared cupcake liners, filling each about 3/4 full.

5. Bake in the preheated oven for 18-20 minutes, or until a toothpick inserted into the center of a cupcake comes out clean. Allow the cupcakes to cool in the tin for 5 minutes before transferring them to a wire rack to cool completely.

- 1 ½ cups all-purpose GF flour
- 1/4 cup unsweetened cocoa powder
- 1 tsp. baking soda
- 1/2 tsp. salt
- 1 cup granulated sugar
- 1/3 cup vegetable oil
- 1 large ripe banana, mashed
- 1 cup water
- 1 tsp. vanilla extract
- 1 Tbsp. vinegar (white or apple cider)
- 1/2 cup chocolate chips (ensure GF)

 (per serving): Calories: 210, Protein: 3g, Carbohydrates: 35g, Fat: 7g, Fiber: 2g, Sugar: 20g

Top it with GF frosting or dusted with powdered sugar for extra sweetness and presentation. For a more intense chocolate flavor, consider using ripe bananas as they lend additional sweetness and moisture to the cupcakes.

Triple Chocolate Avocado Cookies

1. Preheat your oven to 350°F and line a baking sheet with parchment paper.

2. In a large mixing bowl, combine the mashed avocados and coconut sugar. Add the eggs and vanilla extract, mixing until well combined. In a separate bowl, whisk together the gluten-free flour, cocoa powder, baking soda, salt, and espresso powder. Gradually add the dry ingredients to the wet ingredients, stirring until just combined.

3. Fold in the chocolate chips and dark chocolate chunks until evenly distributed throughout the batter.

4. Drop spoonfuls of the batter onto the prepared baking sheet, spacing them about 2 inches apart.

5. Bake in the preheated oven for 10-12 minutes or until the cookies are set on the edges but still soft in the center. Allow the cookies to cool on the baking sheet for 5 minutes before transferring them to a wire rack to cool completely.

15 mn

12 mn

6*

*24 cookies

2 medium ripe avocados, mashed until smooth
1/2 cup coconut sugar (or any sugar)
2 large eggs
1 tsp. vanilla extract
1 cup all-purpose GF flour
1/2 cup unsweetened cocoa powder
1 tsp. baking soda
1/2 tsp. salt
1 tsp. espresso powder (optional)
1 cup semisweet chocolate chips (ensure GF)
1/2 cup dark chocolate chunks (ensure GF)

 (per serving): Calories: 150, Protein: 2g, Carbohydrates: 18g, Fat: 8g, Fiber: 3g Sugar: 10g

 Use avocados that are just ripe to ensure they mash smoothly and mix well into the batter. For an extra chocolatey experience, you can drizzle melted chocolate over the cooled cookies or add a sprinkle of sea salt on top before baking for a sweet and salty twist.

Chocolate Brownies

1. Preheat your oven to 350°F. Grease an 8-inch square baking dish or line it with parchment paper. In a large mixing bowl, combine the pureed avocados and sugar. Beat in the eggs one at a time, then stir in the vanilla extract.

2. Sift together the cocoa powder, gluten-free flour, baking powder, and salt. Gradually add these dry ingredients to the avocado mixture, mixing until well blended.

3. Fold in the chocolate chips, then pour the batter into the prepared baking dish. Spread evenly with a spatula. Bake in the preheated oven for 20-25 minutes, or until a toothpick inserted into the center comes out with a few moist crumbs. Be careful not to overbake to ensure the brownies stay moist and fudgy. Allow the brownies to cool in the pan for about 10 minutes before cutting into squares. Serve warm or at room temperature.

15 mn

25 mn

16

· 2 large ripe avocados, pureed until smooth
· 1 cup granulated sugar (or an equivalent)
· 2 large eggs
· 1 tsp. vanilla extract
· 3/4 cup unsweetened cocoa powder
· 1/2 cup all-purpose GF flour
· 1 tsp. baking powder (ensure GF)
· 1/4 tsp. salt
· 1 cup chocolate chips (ensure GF)

 (per serving): Calories: 180, Protein: 3g, Carbohydrates: 25g, Fat: 9g, Fiber: 3g, Sugar: 17g

 Adding a pinch of espresso powder can enhance the chocolate flavor without making the brownies taste like coffee.

20 mn

50 mn

8-10

1. Preheat your oven to 325°F. Grease and flour a 9-inch round cake pan, ensuring to use gluten-free flour for dusting. In a large mixing bowl, whisk together the gluten-free flour, almond flour, baking powder, baking soda, salt, cinnamon, nutmeg, and cloves.

2. In a separate bowl, mix the applesauce, honey, vegetable oil, eggs, and vanilla extract until well combined. Gradually add the wet ingredients to the dry ingredients, stirring just until blended. Fold in the chopped apples and walnuts, if using.

3. Pour the batter into the prepared cake pan, smoothing the top with a spatula. Bake in the preheated oven for 45-50 minutes, or until a toothpick inserted into the center comes out clean.

4. Allow the cake to cool in the pan for 10 minutes, then turn it out onto a wire rack to cool completely. Once cooled, drizzle the top of the cake with additional honey before serving.

- 1 1/2 cups all-purpose GF flour
- 3/4 cup almond flour
- 1 1/2 tsp. baking powder (ensure GF)
- 1/2 tsp. baking soda
- 1/4 tsp. salt
- 1 tsp. ground cinnamon
- 1/2 tsp. ground nutmeg
- 1/4 tsp. ground cloves
- 3/4 cup unsweetened applesauce
- 1/2 cup honey, plus extra for drizzling
- 1/2 cup vegetable oil
- 3 large eggs
- 1 tsp. vanilla extract
- 2 medium apples, peeled, cored, and chopped
- 1/2 cup walnuts, chopped (optional)

 (per serving): Calories: 310, Protein: 5g, Carbohydrates: 45g, Fat: 14g, Fiber: 3g, Sugar: 26g

 Choosing the right apples is key. For baking, varieties like Granny Smith or Honeycrisp offer a nice balance of tartness and sweetness and hold up well under heat.

Caramelized Apple and Cinnamon Galette

 30 mn

 35 mn

 8

1. To make the pastry dough, combine the gluten-free flour, salt, and sugar in a large bowl. Add the cold butter and use a pastry blender or your fingers to mix until the mixture resembles coarse crumbs. Gradually add ice water, stirring until the dough begins to come together. Form into a disc, wrap in plastic wrap, and chill for at least 1 hour.

2. Preheat your oven to 375°F (190°C). Line a baking sheet with parchment paper.

3. For the filling, melt the butter in a large skillet over medium heat. Add the sliced apples, brown sugar, cinnamon, lemon juice, vanilla extract, and a pinch of salt. Cook, stirring occasionally, until the apples are tender and caramelized, about 10 minutes. Remove from heat and let cool slightly.

4. On a lightly floured surface, roll out the chilled dough into a 12-inch circle. Transfer to the prepared baking sheet. Arrange the caramelized apple mixture in the center of the dough, leaving a 2-inch border. Fold the edges of the dough over the apples, pleating as needed.

5. Brush the dough with the beaten egg and sprinkle the granulated sugar over the apples and the dough. Bake in the preheated oven for 35 minutes, or until the crust is golden brown and the filling is bubbly. Let the galette cool slightly before slicing and serving.

For the Gluten-Free Pastry Dough:
- 1 ½ cups all-purpose GF flour, plus extra for dusting
- 1/2 tsp. salt
- 1/2 tsp. granulated sugar
- 1/2 cup (1 stick) cold unsalted butter, cut into small pieces
- 4-6 Tbsp. ice water

For the Filling:
- 4 medium apples, peeled, cored, and thinly sliced
- ¼ cup unsalted butter
- ½ cup brown sugar
- 1 tsp. ground cinnamon
- 1 Tbsp. lemon juice
- 1 tsp. vanilla extract
- A pinch of salt

For Finishing:
- 1 egg, beaten (for egg wash)
- 2 Tbsp. granulated sugar (for sprinkling)

 (per serving): Calories: 320, Protein: 3g, Carbohydrates: 45g, Fat: 15g, Fiber: 3g, Sugar: 25g

 For a beautifully flaky crust, keep the butter and water as cold as possible when making the dough.

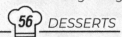

Low-Sugar Pumpkin Muffins

1. Preheat your oven to 350°F and line a 12-cup muffin tin with paper liners or lightly grease with oil.

2. In a large mixing bowl, whisk together the GF flour, granulated sweetener, baking powder, baking soda, salt, cinnamon, nutmeg, ginger, and cloves. In another bowl, mix the pumpkin puree, almond milk, vegetable oil, eggs, and vanilla extract until well combined.

3. Gradually add the wet ingredients to the dry ingredients, stirring until just combined and there are no lumps. Avoid overmixing to ensure the muffins stay light and fluffy. Divide the batter evenly among the muffin cups, filling each about 3/4 full. Bake in the preheated oven for 18-20 minutes, or until a toothpick inserted into the center of a muffin comes out clean.

4. Allow the muffins to cool in the tin for 5 minutes before transferring them to a wire rack to cool completely.

15 mn

20 mn

12

- 1 3/4 cups all-purpose GF flour
- 1/4 cup granulated sweetener of choice
- 1 tsp. baking powder (ensure GF)
- 1/2 tsp. baking soda
- 1/4 tsp. salt
- 2 tsp. ground cinnamon
- 1/2 tsp. ground nutmeg
- 1/4 tsp. ground ginger
- 1/4 tsp. ground cloves
- 1 cup pumpkin puree (not pumpkin pie filling)
- 1/2 cup unsweetened almond milk
- 1/4 cup vegetable oil
- 2 large eggs
- 1 tsp. vanilla extract

 (per serving): Calories: 120, Protein: 3g, Carbohydrates: 18g, Fat: 5g, Fiber: 3g Sugar: 2g

 For added texture and nutrition, consider folding in a handful of chopped nuts or seeds into the batter. These muffins are naturally moist and flavorful from the pumpkin, but make sure to measure your pumpkin puree accurately to avoid overly wet batter.

Lavender and Honey Glazed Lemon Muffins

1. Preheat your oven to 350°F and line a 12-cup muffin tin with paper liners. In a large mixing bowl, whisk together the gluten-free flour, granulated sugar, poppy seeds, chopped lavender, baking powder, baking soda, and salt. In another bowl, beat the eggs lightly, then stir in the Greek yogurt, milk, melted butter, lemon zest, lemon juice, and honey until well combined. Gradually add the wet ingredients to the dry ingredients, stirring just until combined and the batter is smooth.

2. Divide the batter evenly among the prepared muffin cups, filling each about 3/4 full.

3. Bake in the preheated oven for 22-25 minutes, or until a toothpick inserted into the center of a muffin comes out clean. Let the muffins cool in the pan for 5 minutes, then transfer them to a wire rack to cool completely. While the muffins are cooling, prepare the honey-lemon glaze by whisking together the powdered sugar, lemon juice, and honey in a small bowl until smooth.

4. Once the muffins have cooled, drizzle them with the honey-lemon glaze and sprinkle a few dried lavender flowers on top for garnish. Allow the glaze to set before serving.

20 mn

25 mn

12

- 2 cups all-purpose GF flour
- 3/4 cup granulated sugar
- 1 Tbsp. poppy seeds
- 1 Tbsp. dried lavender flowers, finely chopped
- 2 tsp. baking powder
- 1/2 tsp. baking soda
- 1/2 tsp. salt
- 2 large eggs
- 1 cup plain Greek yogurt
- 1/4 cup milk
- 1/2 cup unsalted butter, melted
- 1 Tbsp. lemon zest
- 1/4 cup lemon juice
- 1/4 cup honey

For the Honey-Lemon Glaze:
- 1 cup powdered sugar, sifted (ensure GF)
- 2 Tbsp. lemon juice
- 1 tablespoon honey
- 1/2 teaspoon dried lavender flowers (finely chopped)

 (per serving): Calories: 220, Protein: 4g, Carbohydrates: 38g, Fat: 6g, Fiber: 1g, Sugar: 24g

 The consistency of the glaze can be adjusted by adding more powdered sugar or lemon juice as needed. It should be thick enough to coat the back of a spoon.

Strawberry Dust Meringues

15 mn

90 mn*

12

*plus drying time
- 4 large egg whites, at room temperature
- 1 cup granulated sweetener of choice
- 1/2 tsp. cream of tartar
- 1 tsp. vanilla extract
- 1/2 cup freeze-dried strawberries, pulverized into a fine dust

1. Preheat your oven to 200°F. Line a baking sheet with parchment paper.

2. In a large, clean bowl, beat the egg whites with an electric mixer on medium speed until foamy. Add the cream of tartar and continue to beat, gradually increasing the speed to high, until soft peaks form.

3. Gradually add the granulated sweetener, about a tablespoon at a time, continuing to beat until the mixture forms stiff, glossy peaks. This process should take about 7-10 minutes. Gently fold in the vanilla extract. Using a sieve, gently sift half of the strawberry dust over the meringue mixture, folding it in carefully to maintain the airiness of the meringue.

4. Spoon or pipe the meringue into 12 equal-sized dollops on the prepared baking sheet. Dust the tops of the meringues with the remaining strawberry dust. Bake in the preheated oven for 1 hour and 30 minutes, or until the meringues are dry to the touch and can easily be lifted off the paper without sticking. Turn off the oven and let the meringues sit inside with the door slightly ajar for an additional hour to dry out further.

5. Remove the meringues from the oven and cool completely on the baking sheet before serving or storing.

 (per serving): Calories: 40, Protein: 2g, Carbohydrates: 8g, Fat: 0g, Fiber: 0g, Sugar: 1g

Ensure your mixing bowl and beaters are completely grease-free before starting, as any fat can prevent the egg whites from whipping properly. For a colorful variation, divide the meringue mixture into separate bowls and fold in different freeze-dried fruit powders before baking.

Sugar-Free Coconut Panna Cotta

10 mn

5 mn*

4

*plus 4 hours for chilling
- 1 can (13.5 oz) full-fat coconut milk
- 1/4 cup granulated sweetener of choice
- 2 tsp. gelatin powder
- 1/2 cup boiling water
- 1 tsp. vanilla extract
- Fresh berries or unsweetened shredded coconut for garnish (optional)

1. In a small bowl, sprinkle the gelatin over the boiling water and let it sit for about 5 minutes to soften.

2. In a saucepan, combine the coconut milk and granulated sweetener. Warm the mixture over medium heat, stirring until the sweetener is completely dissolved. Do not allow the mixture to boil.

3. Add the softened gelatin to the coconut milk mixture and stir until the gelatin is fully dissolved. Remove from heat and stir in the vanilla extract.

4. Divide the mixture evenly among 4 serving glasses or ramekins. Allow to cool to room temperature, then cover and refrigerate for at least 4 hours, or until set. Garnish with fresh berries or a sprinkle of unsweetened shredded coconut before serving, if desired.

 (per serving): Calories: 200, Protein: 2g, Carbohydrates: 3g, Fat: 19g, Fiber: 0g, Sugar: 1g

For a smoother panna cotta, you can blend the coconut milk mixture for a few seconds before adding the gelatin. If you prefer a layered dessert, let the first layer set partially in the refrigerator before adding a second layer of flavored panna cotta or fruit puree. To easily unmold the panna cotta, dip the bottom of each ramekin in hot water for a few seconds before inverting onto a serving plate.

Strawberry Cheesecake

1. Preheat your oven to 350°F and grease a 9-inch springform pan. For the crust, combine the almond flour, melted butter, sweetener, and vanilla extract in a bowl. Press the mixture firmly into the bottom of the prepared pan. Bake for 10 minutes, then allow to cool.

2. For the filling, beat the cream cheese and sweetener together until smooth. Add the eggs one at a time, mixing well after each addition. Mix in the sour cream, vanilla extract, lemon juice, and gluten-free flour until just combined. Pour the filling over the cooled crust.

3. Bake for 50 minutes, or until the center is set but slightly jiggly. Turn off the oven, open the oven door slightly, and allow the cheesecake to cool in the oven for 1 hour to prevent cracking.

4. For the strawberry topping, combine the strawberries, sweetener, lemon juice, and vanilla extract in a saucepan over medium heat. Cook until the strawberries are soft. Mix the cornstarch with water and stir into the strawberry mixture. Cook until thickened, then cool slightly. Once both the cheesecake and strawberry topping are cooled, spread the topping over the cheesecake. Refrigerate for at least 4 hours, or overnight, until fully set. Serve chilled, garnished with additional fresh strawberries if desired.

30 mn

60 mn*

8-10

*plus 4 hours for chilling or overnight

For the Crust:
- 1 1/2 cups almond flour
- 1/4 cup unsalted butter, melted
- 3 Tbsp. granulated sweetener of choice
- 1/2 tsp. vanilla extract

For the Filling:
- 2 cups cream cheese, at room temperature
- 1/2 cup granulated sweetener of choice
- 2 large eggs, at room temperature

- 1/2 cup sour cream
- 1 tsp. vanilla extract
- 1 Tbsp. lemon juice
- 1 Tbsp. all-purpose GF flour

For the Strawberry Topping:
- 2 cups fresh strawberries, hulled and sliced
- 1/4 cup granulated sweetener of choice
- 1 tsp. lemon juice
- 1/2 tsp. vanilla extract
- 2 Tbsp. water
- 1 tsp. cornstarch (ensure GF)

 (per serving): Calories: 300, Protein: 7g, Carbohydrates: 10g, Fat: 27g, Fiber: 2g Sugar: 5g

 Water bath baking is not required with the slow cooling method described, but if you're familiar with water baths and prefer using one, it can provide additional protection against cracking.

Peanut Butter Fudge

1. Line an 8x8-inch baking pan with parchment paper, allowing the paper to overhang on two opposite sides for easy removal. In a medium saucepan over low heat, melt together the peanut butter and coconut oil, stirring until smooth and well combined.

2. Remove the saucepan from heat and stir in the granulated sweetener, vanilla extract, and salt until everything is fully incorporated. Pour the mixture into the prepared baking pan, smoothing the top with a spatula. Refrigerate for at least 2 hours, or until the fudge is firm and set.

3. Lift the fudge out of the pan using the overhanging parchment paper. Cut into 16 squares.

4. Serve immediately, or store in an airtight container in the refrigerator for up to 2 weeks.

10 mn*

0 mn

16

*plus 2 hours for chilling

- 2 cups creamy peanut butter
- 1/2 cup coconut oil
- 1/3 cup granulated sweetener of choice
- 1 tsp. vanilla extract
- A pinch of salt (omit if peanut butter is already salted)

 (per serving): Calories: 200, Protein: 6g, Carbohydrates: 8g, Fat: 18g, Fiber: 2g, Sugar: 2g

 For a smoother fudge, you can blend the mixture in a food processor or blender before pouring it into the baking pan. Feel free to add mix-ins to the fudge before setting, such as chopped nuts, chocolate chips or a swirl of sugar-free jam for a fruity twist. If you prefer a firmer texture, you can store the fudge in the freezer. Let it sit at room temperature for a few minutes before cutting and serving for the best flavor and texture.

Oatmeal and Cranberry Cookies

 16 mn

12 mn

 6*

*24 cookies

- 1 3/4 cups GF rolled oats
- 1 cup all-purpose GF flour
- 1/2 tsp. baking soda
- 1/2 tsp. salt
- 1/2 tsp. cinnamon
- 1/2 cup unsalted butter, softened
- 1/4 cup granulated sweetener of choice
- 1/4 cup brown sugar
- 2 large eggs
- 1 teaspoon vanilla extract
- 1/2 cup dried cranberries
- 1/2 cup chopped nuts

1. Preheat your oven to 350°F and line two baking sheets with parchment paper. In a medium bowl, whisk together the rolled oats, gluten-free flour, baking soda, salt, and cinnamon.

2. In a large bowl, use an electric mixer to cream together the butter, granulated sweetener, and brown sugar until light and fluffy. Beat in the eggs one at a time, then stir in the vanilla extract.

3. Gradually mix the dry ingredients into the wet ingredients until well combined. Fold in the dried cranberries and chopped nuts, if using. Drop tablespoonfuls of the cookie dough onto the prepared baking sheets, spacing them about 2 inches apart.

4. Bake in the preheated oven for 10-12 minutes or until the edges are golden and the centers are set.

5. Allow the cookies to cool on the baking sheets for 5 minutes before transferring them to wire racks to cool completely

(per serving): Calories: 100, Protein: 2g, Carbohydrates: 12g, Fat: 5g, Fiber: 1g, Sugar: 2g

For a variation, you can substitute the dried cranberries with other dried fruits like raisins, chopped dates, or dried cherries.

Blueberry Yogurt Swirl Popsicles

 15 mn*

0 mn

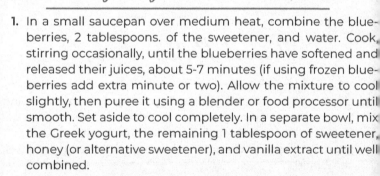 8

*plus 4 hours for freezing

- 2 cups fresh or frozen blueberries
- 3 Tbsp. granulated sweetener of choice
- 1 Tbsp. water
- 2 cups plain Greek yogurt
- 2 Tbsp. honey or a sweetener of choice
- 1 tsp. vanilla extract

1. In a small saucepan over medium heat, combine the blueberries, 2 tablespoons. of the sweetener, and water. Cook, stirring occasionally, until the blueberries have softened and released their juices, about 5-7 minutes (if using frozen blueberries add extra minute or two). Allow the mixture to cool slightly, then puree it using a blender or food processor until smooth. Set aside to cool completely. In a separate bowl, mix the Greek yogurt, the remaining 1 tablespoon of sweetener, honey (or alternative sweetener), and vanilla extract until well combined.

2. To assemble the popsicles, spoon a layer of the yogurt mixture into the bottom of each popsicle mold. Add a layer of the blueberry puree on top, then continue to alternate between the yogurt and blueberry layers until the molds are filled. Use a skewer or the handle of a spoon to gently swirl the layers together for a marbled effect.

3. Insert popsicle sticks into the molds, then freeze for at least 4 hours, or until the popsicles are firm.

4. To release the popsicles from the molds, run warm water over the outside of the molds for a few seconds, then gently pull the popsicles out.

For a creamier popsicle, you can blend some of the yogurt mixture with the blueberry puree before layering. Experiment with different fruit and yogurt flavors to create your own custom popsicle variations. Strawberry, raspberry, and peach all make excellent substitutes or additions to the blueberries.

(per serving): Calories: 100, Protein: 5g, Carbohydrates: 12g, Fat: 2g, Fiber: 1g, Sugar: 9g

 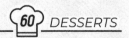

Banana and Peanut Butter Ice Cream

1. Place the frozen banana slices in a food processor or high-powered blender. Blend until they reach a smooth and creamy consistency, scraping down the sides as needed.

2. Add the peanut butter, vanilla extract, and a pinch of salt to the blended bananas. Continue to blend until all the ingredients are well incorporated and the mixture is smooth.

3. For soft-serve consistency, serve the ice cream immediately, garnished with your choice of optional toppings. For a firmer ice cream, transfer the mixture to a freezer-safe container and freeze for at least 2 hours or until it reaches your desired consistency.

4. Before serving, let the ice cream sit at room temperature for a few minutes to soften slightly, making it easier to scoop. Serve with your choice of toppings for added texture and flavor.

10 mn*

0 mn

4

*plus freezing time

- 4 ripe bananas, peeled, sliced, and frozen
- 1/4 cup creamy peanut butter
- 1/2 tsp. vanilla extract
- A pinch of salt
- Optional toppings: chopped nuts, dark chocolate chips, or a drizzle of peanut butter

 (per serving): Calories: 200, Protein: 4g, Carbohydrates: 27g, Fat: 10g, Fiber: 3g Sugar: 14g

 Ensure the bananas are very ripe before freezing them, as this will naturally sweeten the ice cream without the need for added sugars. If you have difficulty blending the bananas, add a tablespoon of almond milk or another plant-based milk to help the blending process without significantly altering the flavor. Experiment with add-ins by blending in cocoa powder for a chocolate version or mixing in cinnamon for added warmth and spice.

Chocolate Peanut Butter Cookie Cups

 20 mn

 12 mn*

1. Preheat your oven to 350°F. Grease a 12-cup mini muffin tin or line with mini muffin liners.

2. In a bowl, whisk together the gluten-free flour, cocoa powder, baking soda, and salt.

3. In a separate bowl, beat together the butter, granulated sweetener, and brown sugar until light and fluffy. Add the egg and vanilla extract, mixing well. Gradually mix the dry ingredients into the wet ingredients until well combined. The dough will be thick.

4. Divide the dough evenly among the prepared muffin cups, pressing gently to form a cup shape. Bake for 10-12 minutes or until set. Remove from the oven and immediately use a spoon to press down the center of each cookie cup to create a well. Allow to cool in the pan for 10 minutes before transferring to a wire rack to cool completely.

5. For the filling, beat together the peanut butter, sweetener, heavy cream, and vanilla extract until smooth and creamy. Once the cookie cups are cool, spoon or pipe the peanut butter filling into the wells of each cookie cup. Refrigerate the cookie cups for at least 20 minutes to set the filling before serving.

 12

*plus 30 minutes for cooling

For the Cookie Cups:
- 1 cup all-purpose GF flour
- 1/2 cup unsweetened cocoa powder
- 1/2 tsp. baking soda
- 1/4 tsp. salt
- 1/2 cup unsalted butter, softened
- 1/2 cup granulated sweetener of choice
- 1/4 cup brown sugar

- 1 large egg
- 1 tsp. vanilla extract

For the Peanut Butter Filling:
- 3/4 cup creamy peanut butter
- 1/4 cup granulated sweetener of choice
- 1/4 cup heavy cream
- 1/2 tsp. vanilla extract

 (per serving): Calories: 250, Protein: 6g, Carbohydrates: 18g, Fat: 18g, Fiber: 2g, Sugar: 1g

 For an extra chocolatey touch, you can melt sugar-free chocolate chips and drizzle over the filled cookie cups before refrigerating. Ensure all ingredients for the filling are at room temperature to achieve a smooth, creamy texture.

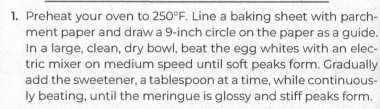

Pavlova

20 mn

90 mn*

8

1. Preheat your oven to 250°F. Line a baking sheet with parchment paper and draw a 9-inch circle on the paper as a guide. In a large, clean, dry bowl, beat the egg whites with an electric mixer on medium speed until soft peaks form. Gradually add the sweetener, a tablespoon at a time, while continuously beating, until the meringue is glossy and stiff peaks form.

2. Fold in the vinegar, cornstarch, and vanilla extract gently with a spatula until just combined.

3. Spoon the meringue onto the parchment paper, using the circle as a guide. Shape the meringue into a round base with a slight well in the center, so the edges are higher than the middle.

4. Bake in the preheated oven for 1 hour and 30 minutes, or until the meringue is crisp and dry. Turn off the oven and let the meringue cool completely inside the oven with the door slightly ajar. This prevents cracking. For the topping, beat the heavy whipping cream, sweetener, and vanilla extract in a bowl until soft peaks form. Once the meringue base is cooled, carefully transfer it to a serving plate. Spoon the whipped cream over the meringue base and top with fresh fruit.

5. Serve immediately after assembling to ensure the meringue base remains crisp.

*plus 1 hour for cooling

For the Meringue Base:
- 4 large egg whites, at room temperature
- 1 cup granulated sweetener of choice
- 1 tsp. white vinegar
- 1 tsp. cornstarch (ensure GF)
- 1 tsp. vanilla extract

For the Topping:
- 1 cup heavy whipping cream
- 2 Tbsp. granulated sweetener of choice
- 1 tsp. vanilla extract
- Fresh fruit for topping

 (per serving): Calories: 180, Protein: 2g, Carbohydrates: 10g, Fat: 14g, Fiber: 0g, Sugar: 2g

Ensure your mixing bowl and beaters are completely grease-free before starting, as any fat can prevent the egg whites from forming stiff peaks. Experiment with different toppings according to season and availability. Mango and passion fruit make for a deliciously tropical Pavlova, while mixed berries offer a classic variation.

Coconut and Mango Chia Pudding

15 mn*

0 mn

4

1. In a large bowl, whisk together the coconut milk, chia seeds, sweetener, and vanilla extract until well combined. Divide the mixture evenly among four serving glasses or jars.

2. Cover and refrigerate overnight, or at least 6 hours, until the chia seeds have absorbed the liquid and the pudding has thickened. Before serving, blend the mango cubes in a blender until smooth to create a mango puree. Layer the mango puree over the set chia pudding in each serving glass or jar.

3. Garnish with unsweetened shredded coconut and additional cubed mango on top. Serve chilled as a delicious and healthy breakfast or dessert.

*plus overnight soaking

- 1 can (13.5 oz) full-fat coconut milk
- 1/4 cup chia seeds
- 2 Tbsp. granulated sweetener of choice
- 1 tsp. vanilla extract
- 1 ripe mango, peeled and cubed
- Unsweetened shredded coconut, for garnish
- Additional cubed mango, for garnish

 (per serving): Calories: 280, Protein: 3g, Carbohydrates: 15g, Fat: 24g, Fiber: 5g, Sugar: 8g

 If you prefer a thinner pudding, add a bit more coconut milk or a splash of almond milk to adjust the consistency before refrigerating.

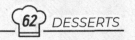

Chocolate Coconut Almond Tart

1. For the crust, combine almond flour, cocoa powder, melted coconut oil, sweetener, vanilla extract, and a pinch of salt in a mixing bowl. Stir until the mixture comes together and resembles wet sand.

2. Press the crust mixture firmly into the bottom and up the sides of a 9-inch tart pan with a removable bottom. Place in the freezer to set while preparing the filling, about 10 minutes.

3. For the filling, heat the coconut milk in a saucepan over medium heat until it starts to simmer. Do not let it boil. Remove from heat and add the finely chopped dark chocolate, sweetener, vanilla extract, and a pinch of salt. Let it sit for a minute, then stir until smooth and the chocolate has completely melted. Pour the chocolate filling into the prepared crust and refrigerate until set, about 2 hours or overnight. Before serving, sprinkle the top of the tart with toasted sliced almonds and shredded coconut for garnish. Serve chilled. The tart can be stored in the refrigerator for up to 4 days.

 30 mn*

 0 mn

 8-10

*plus 2 hour for chilling

For the Crust:
- 1 1/2 cups almond flour
- 1/4 cup unsweetened cocoa powder
- 1/4 cup coconut oil, melted
- 2 Tbsp. granulated sweetener of choice
- 1 tsp. vanilla extract
- A pinch of salt

For the Filling:
- 1 can (13.5 oz) full-fat coconut milk

- 7 oz. dark chocolate, finely chopped
- 1/4 cup granulated sweetener of choice
- 1 tsp. vanilla extract
- A pinch of salt

For the Topping:
- 1/2 cup sliced almonds, toasted
- 1/4 cup unsweetened shredded coconut, toasted

 (per serving): Calories: 350, Protein: 6g, Carbohydrates: 15g, Fat: 30g, Fiber: 5g Sugar: 5g

 Make sure all ingredients are at room temperature for easier mixing and to prevent coconut oil from solidifying when mixed with other ingredients. For a smoother filling, strain the coconut milk mixture to remove any potential lumps before adding the chocolate. The tart can also be frozen for a firmer texture..

Coconut Macaroons

1. Preheat your oven to 325°F and line a baking sheet with parchment paper. In a large bowl, whisk together the egg whites, sweetener, vanilla extract, and salt until well combined and slightly frothy.

2. Fold in the shredded coconut until the mixture is well coated and holds together.

3. sing a tablespoon or a small ice cream scoop, drop the mixture onto the prepared baking sheet, forming small mounds. Leave some space between each macaroon as they will spread a little.

4. Bake in the preheated oven for 20-25 minutes, or until the edges and tops are golden brown.

5. Remove from the oven and let the macaroons cool on the baking sheet for 5 minutes before transferring them to a wire rack to cool completely.

 15 mn

 20 mn

 24

- 4 large egg whites
- 1/2 cup granulated sweetener of choice
- 1 tsp. vanilla extract
- 1/4 tsp. salt
- 4 cups unsweetened shredded coconut

 (per serving): Calories: 100, Protein: 1g, Carbohydrates: 4g, Fat: 9g, Fiber: 2g, Sugar: 1g

 These coconut macaroons can be dipped in melted dark chocolate after they have cooled for an extra decadent treat. For a zesty variation, add the zest of one lemon or lime to the mixture before baking. This will add a refreshing citrus note to the macaroons.

· 8 oz. high-quality GF dark chocolate, chopped
· 1 cup heavy cream
· 2 Tbsp. sugar (optional)
· 1 tsp. vanilla extract
· A pinch of salt

For dipping:
· Fresh strawberries, whole or halved
· Banana slices
· GF cake pieces, cubed
· Marshmallows
· Pineapple chunks
· Any other fruit or GF goodies you love

10 mn
10 mn
2-4

 (per serving, chocolate only):
Calories: 550, Protein: 5g, Carbohydrates: 45g, Fat: 40g, Fiber: 5g, Sugar: 35g

Valentine's Day Chocolate Fondue

1. In a medium saucepan, heat the heavy cream over medium heat until it begins to simmer. Do not let it boil. Once simmering, reduce the heat to low and add the chopped chocolate, sugar (if using), vanilla extract, and a pinch of salt. Stir continuously until the chocolate has completely melted and the mixture is smooth.

2. Transfer the chocolate mixture to a fondue pot and keep warm over a low flame or candle. If you don't have a fondue pot, you can serve the fondue in a heatproof bowl; just be sure to enjoy it before it cools and thickens.

3. Arrange the dipping ingredients on a platter around the fondue pot. Use fondue forks, skewers, or regular forks to dip the items into the chocolate mixture. Enjoy the rich, romantic chocolate fondue with your Valentine, dipping and delighting in your favorite treats.

 Choosing a high-quality gluten-free dark chocolate is key to achieving the best flavor for your fondue. Look for chocolate with a cocoa content of at least 60% for a rich and satisfying taste. Remember to cut the fruits and cake pieces into bite-sized portions for easy dipping.

· 4 large potatoes, peeled and grated
· 1 small onion, grated
· 2 large eggs, beaten
· 1/4 cup GF all-purpose flour
· 1 tsp. salt
· 1/2 tsp. black pepper
· Olive oil or vegetable oil, for frying
· For serving: applesauce and/or sour cream

20 mn
30 mn
4-6

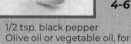

 (per serving, without applesauce or sour cream):
Calories: 250, Protein: 6g, Carbohydrates: 40g, Fat: 8g, Fiber: 5g, Sugar: 3g

Gluten-Free Latkes for Hanukkah

1. Place the grated potatoes in a clean cloth or cheesecloth and squeeze out as much moisture as possible. In a large bowl, mix together the squeezed potatoes, grated onion, beaten eggs, gluten-free flour, salt, and pepper until well combined.

2. Heat a large skillet over medium-high heat and add enough oil to coat the bottom of the pan generously. Form the potato mixture into patties, about 3 inches in diameter. Fry the latkes in batches, without crowding the skillet, for 3-4 minutes on each side or until golden brown and crispy.

3. Transfer the cooked latkes to a paper towel-lined plate to drain any excess oil. Serve hot with a side of applesauce and/or sour cream.

 Removing as much moisture as possible from the potatoes is key to achieving crispy latkes. For a lighter version, the latkes can be baked in a preheated oven at 425°F for 12-15 minutes on each side, or until golden and crispy. Gluten-free flour can be substituted with potato starch for a slightly different texture and taste.

Gluten-Free Pumpkin Pie

1. Preheat your oven to 350°F. To make the crust, combine the gluten-free flour and salt in a large bowl. Add the butter and use your fingers or a pastry blender to mix until the mixture resembles coarse crumbs. Stir in the egg and just enough cold water to form a dough. Wrap in plastic wrap and chill for 30 minutes. Roll the dough between two pieces of parchment paper to fit a 9-inch pie plate. Transfer to the pie plate, trim the edges, and prick the bottom with a fork.

2. For the filling, in a large bowl, whisk together the pumpkin puree, sugar, salt, cinnamon, ginger, cloves, and nutmeg. Add the eggs, cream, and vanilla, and whisk until smooth. Pour the filling into the prepared crust and smooth the top with a spatula.

3. Bake in the preheated oven for 55 minutes, or until the filling is set but slightly wobbly in the center. Let the pie cool completely on a wire rack, about 2 hours, before serving. Serve with a dollop of whipped cream on top.

20 mn

55 mn*

8

*plus 2 hours foor cooling

For the crust:
- 1 1/4 cups GF all-purpose flour
- 1/4 tsp. salt
- 6 Tbsp. unsalted butter, cold and cubed
- 1 large egg
- 2-4 Tbsp. cold water

For the filling:
- 1 (15 oz) can pumpkin puree

- 3/4 cup granulated sugar
- 1/2 tsp. salt
- 1 tsp. ground cinnamon
- 1/2 tsp. ground ginger
- 1/4 tsp. ground cloves
- 1/8 tsp. ground nutmeg
- 2 large eggs
- 1 cup heavy cream
- 1 tsp. vanilla extract
- Whipped cream, for serving

(per serving): Calories: 320, Protein: 5g, Carbohydrates: 40g, Fat: 16g, Fiber: 2g Sugar: 22g

For a silkier filling, make sure to mix until just combined and smooth. Overmixing can introduce air bubbles, which may cause cracks as the pie bakes. Chill the pie thoroughly before serving to allow the filling to set completely, creating the perfect slice.

Quinoa Stuffed Bell Peppers for Fourth of July

1. In a saucepan, bring the vegetable broth to a boil. Add the quinoa, reduce the heat to low, cover, and simmer for 15 minutes, or until the liquid is absorbed. Remove from heat and let it sit, covered, for 5 minutes. Fluff with a fork. Preheat your grill to medium-high heat for grilling, or your oven to 375°F for baking. Cut the tops off the bell peppers and remove the seeds and membranes. If necessary, slightly trim the bottoms to help them stand upright, but be careful not to create a hole.

2. In a skillet over medium heat, heat the olive oil. Add the onion and garlic, and sauté until soft. Add the zucchini and corn, and cook for another 5 minutes. Stir in the black beans, cooked quinoa, cumin, paprika, salt, and pepper. Cook until everything is heated through. Remove from heat and stir in the cilantro. Stuff the bell peppers with the quinoa mixture and top with cheese if using.

3. If grilling, place the peppers on the grill, and close the lid. Grill for about 15 minutes, or until the peppers are tender and the cheese is melted. If baking, place the peppers in a baking dish, and bake for about 25 minutes. Serve the stuffed peppers with a side of your choice for a festive Fourth of July cookout.

20 mn

25 mn

6

- 6 large bell peppers, a mix of red, light green, and blue purple to fit the Fourth of July theme
- 1 cup quinoa, rinsed
- 2 cups vegetable broth
- 1 Tbsp. olive oil
- 1 small onion, finely chopped
- 2 cloves garlic, minced
- 1 zucchini, diced
- 1 cup corn kernels, fresh or

frozen
- 1 can (15 oz) black beans, drained and rinsed
- 1 tsp. ground cumin
- 1 tsp. paprika
- Salt and pepper, to taste
- 1/2 cup fresh cilantro, chopped
- 1 cup shredded cheese (ensure GF), optional

(per serving): Calories: 220, Protein: 9g, Carbohydrates: 38g, Fat: 5g, Fiber: 8g, Sugar: 7g

To maintain the Fourth of July theme, serve with a side of blue corn chips and a red salsa. Experiment with different vegetables according to season and preference.

New Year's Eve Champagne Cupcakes

⏱ 30 mn

🍳 18 mn

🍴 12

1. Preheat your oven to 350°F and line a 12-cup muffin tin with cupcake liners. In a medium bowl, whisk together the gluten-free flour, baking powder, baking soda, and salt.

2. In a large bowl, beat the softened butter and granulated sugar until light and fluffy. Add the eggs, one at a time, fully incorporating after each addition. Stir in the vanilla extract.

3. Gradually mix in the dry ingredients in three additions, alternating with the sour cream and champagne, starting and ending with the dry ingredients. Mix until just combined.

4. Divide the batter evenly among the prepared muffin cups, filling each about 2/3 full.

5. Bake for 18 minutes, or until a toothpick inserted into the center of a cupcake comes out clean. Allow the cupcakes to cool in the pan for 5 minutes before transferring them to a wire rack to cool completely. For the frosting, beat the softened butter on medium speed until creamy. Gradually add the powdered sugar, champagne, and vanilla extract, beating until smooth and fluffy.

6. Frost the cooled cupcakes and sprinkle with edible glitter or gold sugar to celebrate the New Year with a sparkle.

- 1 3/4 cups GF all-purpose flour
- 1 tsp. baking powder
- 1/2 tsp. baking soda
- 1/4 tsp. salt
- 1/2 cup unsalted butter, softened
- 1 cup granulated sugar
- 2 large eggs
- 1 tsp. vanilla extract
- 1/2 cup sour cream
- 1/2 cup champagne or sparkling wine

For the Frosting:
- 1 cup unsalted butter, softened
- 4 cups powdered sugar
- 1/4 cup champagne or sparkling wie
- 1 tsp vanilla extract
- Edible glitter or gold sugar, for decoration

(per serving, per cupcake, without frosting): Calories: 280, Protein: 3g, Carbohydrates: 45g, Fat: 10g, Fiber: 1g, Sugar: 20g

 Ensure all ingredients, especially the champagne or sparkling wine, are at room temperature to achieve a smooth batter. For a non-alcoholic version, replace the champagne with sparkling grape juice.

Independence Day Berry Trifle

⏱ 30 mn

🍳 20 mn

🍴 8-10

1. Preheat your oven to 350°F. Grease and flour a 9-inch round cake pan. In a large bowl, beat the eggs and sugar together until pale and fluffy. Add the vanilla extract and mix well.

2. Sift together the gluten-free flour and baking powder. Gently fold the dry ingredients into the egg mixture until just combined. Pour the batter into the prepared cake pan and smooth the top. Bake for 20-25 minutes, or until a toothpick inserted into the center comes out clean. Allow to cool completely.

3. In a chilled bowl, beat the heavy cream, powdered sugar, and vanilla extract until stiff peaks form. Be careful not to overbeat. Cut the cooled sponge cake into 1-inch cubes. In a large trifle dish or glass bowl, create a layer of cake cubes at the bottom. Add a layer of whipped cream over the cake, followed by a layer of mixed berries. Repeat the layering process until all ingredients are used, finishing with a layer of berries on top for a patriotic look.

4. Chill the trifle in the refrigerator for at least an hour before serving. This allows the flavors to meld together beautifully.

For the Gluten-Free Sponge Cake:
- 1 cup GF all-purpose flour
- 1 cup sugar
- 4 large eggs
- 1 tsp. vanilla extract
- 1/2 tsp. baking powder

For the Layers:
- 2 cups heavy cream
- 1/4 cup powdered sugar
- 1 tsp. vanilla extract
- 2 cups fresh strawberries, sliced
- 2 cups fresh blueberries
- 1 cup fresh raspberries

(per serving): Calories: 400, Protein: 4g, Carbohydrates: 35g, Fat: 28g, Fiber: 3g, Sugar: 25g

 For a quicker version, GF ladyfingers or pre-made GF sponge cake can be used instead of making the cake from scratch. To keep the berries fresh and prevent them from bleeding into the cream, pat them dry after washing. For an extra touch of flavor, you can sprinkle each layer of cake with a small amount of liqueur or fruit juice.

Easter Lamb with Mint Pesto

1. In a small bowl, mix together olive oil, minced garlic, salt, pepper, rosemary, and thyme. Rub this mixture all over the leg of lamb, ensuring it's well coated. Cover and refrigerate to marinate for at least 2 hours, or overnight for best results. Preheat your oven to 350°F. Place the marinated lamb in a roasting pan, fat side up. Roast in the preheated oven for about 1 hour and 30 minutes, or until a meat thermometer inserted into the thickest part of the meat reads 145°F for medium-rare.

2. While the lamb is roasting, make the mint pesto. Combine mint leaves, parsley, olive oil, Parmesan cheese, nuts, and garlic in a food processor. Pulse until the mixture is finely chopped. Season with salt and pepper to taste. Once the lamb is cooked to your liking, remove it from the oven and let it rest for 10 minutes before carving. This allows the juices to redistribute, ensuring the meat is succulent and moist. Serve the lamb slices with a generous spoonful of mint pesto on the side.

20 mn*

90 mn

6-8

*plus marinating time

For the Lamb:
- 1 bone-in leg of lamb (about 5 to 6 lb.s)
- 2 Tbsp. olive oil
- 4 cloves garlic, minced
- 2 tsp. salt
- 1 tsp. freshly ground black pepper
- 2 tsp. dried rosemary
- 1 tsp. dried thyme

For the Mint Pesto:
- 1 cup fresh mint leaves
- 1/2 cup fresh parsley leaves
- 1/2 cup olive oil
- 1/4 cup grated Parmesan cheese
- 2 Tbsp. pine nuts or walnuts
- 2 cloves garlic
- Salt and pepper, to taste

(per serving): Calories: 690, Protein: 65g, Carbohydrates: 2g, Fat: 46g, Fiber: 1g Sugar: 0g

Marinating the lamb overnight will enhance the flavor and tenderness of the meat. The internal temperature of the lamb will continue to rise a few degrees as it rests, so remove it from the oven when it's a few degrees below your desired doneness.

Roasted Turkey with Gravy

1. Preheat your oven to 325°F. Remove the turkey giblets and neck, rinse the turkey inside and out, and pat dry with paper towels. Season the cavity and outside of the turkey generously with salt and pepper. Drizzle olive oil over the turkey. Stuff the cavity with onion, lemon halves, and fresh herbs.

2. Place the turkey breast-side up on a rack in a large roasting pan. Tuck the wing tips under the body. Pour 2 cups of broth into the bottom of the pan.

3. Tent the turkey with aluminum foil and roast, basting occasionally with the pan juices. About 2/3 through cooking, remove the foil to allow the skin to brown.

4. The turkey is done when a meat thermometer inserted into the thickest part of the thigh reads 165°F. Transfer the turkey to a cutting board, tent it with foil, and let it rest for at least 20 minutes before carving.

5. For the gravy, pour the drippings from the roasting pan into a saucepan, skimming off the excess fat. Stir in the cornstarch or gluten-free flour, whisking until smooth. Add the reserved broth to the saucepan and bring to a simmer, stirring constantly until the gravy thickens. Season with salt and pepper to taste. If the gravy is too thick, thin it with a little water or additional broth.

30 mn

3-4 h*

****

*varies by turkey size
**varies by turkey size

- 1 whole turkey (10 to 12 lb.), thawed if frozen
- Salt and pepper, to taste
- 2 Tbsp. olive oil
- 1 onion, quartered
- 1 lemon, halved
- A few sprigs of fresh thyme, rosemary, and sage
- 4 cups low-sodium chicken or turkey broth (ensure GF)
- 3 Tbsp. cornstarch or GF

all-purpose flour
- Water or additional broth, as needed

For the Gravy:
- Drippings from the roasted turkey
- 3 Tbsp. cornstarch or gluten-free all-purpose flour
- 2 cups reserved turkey or chicken broth

(per serving): Calories: 170 per 100g, Protein: 24g, Carbohydrates: 2g, Fat: 8g, Fiber: 0g, Sugar: 0g

For extra moist and flavorful meat, consider brining your turkey for 12 to 24 hours before roasting. Resting the turkey before carving is crucial for juicy, succulent meat as it allows the juices to redistribute.

Gluten-Free Gingerbread Cookies

25 mn

10 mn

6*

1. In a medium bowl, whisk together the gluten-free flour, baking soda, salt, ginger, cinnamon, cloves, and nutmeg. In a large bowl, beat the butter and brown sugar together until fluffy. Add the egg and molasses, mixing until fully combined.

2. Gradually add the dry ingredients to the wet ingredients, stirring until a dough forms. Divide the dough in half, wrap each half in plastic wrap, and chill in the refrigerator for at least 2 hours or overnight. Preheat your oven to 350°F and line two baking sheets with parchment paper.

3. On a lightly floured surface, roll out one portion of the dough to about 1/4-inch thickness. Using cookie cutters, cut into desired shapes and place on the prepared baking sheets.

4. Bake for 8-10 minutes or until the edges start to brown. Remove from the oven and let cool on the baking sheets for 5 minutes before transferring to a wire rack to cool completely.

5. Once cooled, decorate with icing, sprinkles, and candy as desired.

*24 cookies

- 2 1/4 cups GF all-purpose flour, plus more for rolling
- 1 tsp. baking soda
- 1/4 tsp. salt
- 1 Tbsp. ground ginger
- 1 tsp. ground cinnamon
- 1/2 tsp. ground cloves
- 1/4 tsp. ground nutmeg
- 1/2 cup unsalted butter,
- room temperature
- 3/4 cup dark brown sugar, packed
- 1 large egg
- 1/3 cup unsulfored molasses
- For decorating: GF icing, sprinkles, and candy (optional)

(per cookie, without decorations): Calories: 110, Protein: 1g, Carbohydrates: 20g, Fat: 3g, Fiber: 1g, Sugar: 11g

For a softer cookie, roll the dough out slightly thicker and bake for the shorter recommended time. Decorating these cookies can be a delightful holiday activity for the whole family. Feel free to get creative with gluten-free icing and decorations!

King Cake for Mardi Gras

45 mn*

30 mn

12

1. In the bowl of a stand mixer fitted with a dough hook, combine the gluten-free flour, granulated sugar, instant yeast, xanthan gum (if using), and salt. Add the melted butter, warm milk, eggs, vanilla extract, and lemon zest. Mix on medium speed until a smooth dough forms. The dough will be sticky. Transfer the dough to a lightly floured surface and knead briefly to form a ball. Place in a greased bowl, cover with a damp cloth, and let rise in a warm place for 1 hour, or until doubled in size. Preheat your oven to 350°F and line a baking sheet with parchment paper.

2. Roll out the risen dough into a rectangle, about 1/4-inch thick. Spread the softened butter over the dough, leaving a small margin at the edges. Mix the brown sugar and cinnamon together and sprinkle evenly over the butter.

3. Starting at the long edge, roll the dough tightly into a log. Form the log into a circle on the prepared baking sheet, pinching the ends together to seal. Bake for 30 minutes, or until golden brown. Let cool slightly on a wire rack. For the icing, mix the powdered sugar, milk (or water), and vanilla extract until smooth. Adjust the consistency with more liquid or powdered sugar as needed.

4. Drizzle the icing over the warm cake. Immediately sprinkle the colored sugar in alternating bands of purple, green, and gold around the cake. Serve and don't forget to hide a small, oven-safe figurine inside for someone to find!

*plus 1 hour for dough to rise

For the Dough:
- 2 1/2 cups GF all-purpose flour, plus extra for dusting
- 1/4 cup granulated sugar
- 1 packet (2 1/4 tsp.) instant yeast
- 1 teaspoon xanthan gum (if not included in your flour blend)
- 1/2 teaspoon salt
- 1/4 cup unsalted butter, melted
- 1/2 cup warm milk (110°F)
- 2 large eggs
- 1 tsp. vanilla extract
- Zest of 1 lemon

For the Filling:
- 1/2 cup light brown sugar, packed
- 1 Tbsp. ground cinnamon
- 2 Tbsp. unsalted butter, softened

For the Icing:
- 1 cup powdered sugar
- 1-2 Tbsp. milk or water
- 1/2 tsp. vanilla extract

For the Decoration:
- Purple, green, and gold (yellow) colored sugar

(per serving): Calories: 300, Protein: 4g, Carbohydrates: 50g, Fat: 10g, Fiber: 2g, Sugar: 30g

If you're including a figurine in your King Cake, be sure to notify your guests to avoid any surprises!

Conclusion

As we close this chapter on our gluten-free adventure, I hope you've discovered that this book is so much more than a collection of recipes. It's been crafted as a source of inspiration, a companion to support you on your journey through the challenges and delights of living without gluten.

In these pages, you've not only found delicious recipes but also practical tips, personal stories, and sound advice to keep you motivated. Think of this book as your culinary cheerleader, always on the sidelines, encouraging you to push forward and reminding you of the importance of nurturing yourself in every way.

This journey isn't about restriction; it's about exploration and embracing new tastes and healthier habits that enhance your daily life. Welcome these changes and adapt them to suit your unique needs.

Here's to your gluten-free journey! May it be enriched with tasty meals, joyful memories, and a sense of achievement as you take excellent care of yourself and your loved ones. Every small step is a significant leap towards better health and a fuller life. Set achievable goals to make this lifestyle transition smoother.

I'm thrilled to be part of your flavorful experience! If you found this book helpful, please consider sharing your thoughts in a review on Amazon. Your feedback helps us improve and assists others in finding the guidance they might need. Celebrate your well-being, because that's truly worth a toast!

Diane Romano

Recipe Index

BONUS

1 **GLUTEN FREE BREAD ABC**: Master techniques, tips and recipe that deliver the taste and feel of artisan bread, ensuring you gluten-free loaves are indistinguishable from traditional ones.

2 **GLUTEN FREE AIR FRYER COOKBOOK**: Unlock 50+ easy, health and delicious gluten-free recipes to transform your air fryer into powerhouse for quick, tasty, and nutritious meals every day.

Made in United States
North Haven, CT
16 November 2024